From Strength To Strength

From Strength To Strength

Social Work Education and Aboriginal People

Edited by

Kay Feehan & David Hannis

Grant
MacEwan
Community
College

Published by: Grant MacEwan Community College
             Social Work Program
             P.O. Box 1796
             Edmonton, Alberta, Canada
             T5J 2P2

Copy editing: Cathy Conroy

Cover illustration: Kathy Alexis

Design and production: Kevin Collard, GMCC Media Services

Printed and bound in Canada by: Quality Color Press Inc.

Printed on recycled paper.

Canadian Cataloguing in Publication Data

   Main entry under title:
      From Strength to Strength
      Social Work Education and Aboriginal People

   Includes bibliographical references

   ISBN 0–9697019–0–X

This book is dedicated to:

John Graham Hutton

April 24, 1944 – December 24, 1990

Social Worker, Teacher, and Colleague who
shared a vision of a more just society
and a commitment to
aboriginal social work education.

Contents

Contents

Contents

Foreword

Gerry Kelly

President, Grant MacEwan Community College

One of the roles of a community college is to adapt its programming to meet the needs of particular client groups within the community it serves. By working cooperatively with members of a group with unique needs, a college can serve as a catalyst for community development. It can help people to help themselves.

This book describes the results of an outstanding example of college-community collaboration and the adaptation of a program to meet the needs of a unique client group. For 16 years, Grant MacEwan Community College (GMCC) has been delivering Social Work programs in a variety of rural communities and addressing the expressed needs of aboriginal students, while at the same time ensuring that these courses are transferable to other post-secondary educational institutions. Evaluations of these outreach programs report impressive levels of success from the perspective of the graduates, their employers, and the community leaders.

Gerry Kelly

This book is a collection of essays written by people who have firsthand experience with our Social Work Outreach programs. These essays reflect a variety of perspectives—instructors, students, administrators, and aboriginal and non-aboriginal persons—and deal with issues that range from overall vision and philosophy to practical discussions of instructional methods. As such, this book is likely to be of interest to scholars, social work practitioners, policy analysts, or anyone else involved in delivering post-secondary educational services to aboriginal persons.

I have had the privilege of attending several Social Work Outreach gradua- tions. I was always thrilled to be there. The words in this book express the incredible dedication and caring of both the aboriginal students and the Grant MacEwan fac- ulty. They made ex- traordinary commit- ments to collaborative learning, to generat- ing local community support, and to tailor- ing instruction to suit the time, place, and pace of the aboriginal student. These initia- tives, though not with- out a myriad of prob- lems, have been out- standingly successful.

GMCC President Gerry Kelly with High Level program graduate Mary Francis

The achievements of GMCC's Social Work Outreach programs can be attributed to the determination and courage of the students themselves; to the support given them by their families and communities; to the encouragement provided by the on-site GMCC Coordinators; and to the demonstrated commitment of the GMCC instructors. The program's emphasis on personal growth and development forced many students to confront personal issues that might otherwise have interfered with their future roles as helping professionals. Students often travelled considerable distances to get to class, sometimes under less than ideal weather conditions. Most of our students were also women who refused to abandon their family and community responsibilities in order to concentrate on their studies.

The students weren't the only ones who sacrificed. Driving on Alberta's rural highways in winter, living in small town motels, teaching six hours a day, five days a week for several weeks, preparing for classes, dealing with student concerns, and worrying about families left behind in the city, caused more than one instructor to question his or her sanity.

This book also represents an important but often underrated role of the community college—the role of applied research and scholarship in areas of direct and demonstrable benefit to the community. In documenting their experiences with the Social Work Outreach program, the book's contributors and editors extend the benefits of this program to those beyond their own community. They have become partners in the College's wider circle of communities: provincial, national, and international. To them, and to all the students, instructors, and community leaders, whose skills and determination have contributed to the ongoing success of this program, Congratulations!

G. O. Kelly

Introduction

Beginning the Journey

Kay Feehan & David Hannis

This book is about many journeys. Some began almost two decades ago; others originated more recently. It is a collection of essays by people who have been involved in some capacity with the off-campus Social Work Programs which Grant MacEwan Community College (GMCC) has been offering to aboriginal persons in Alberta, Canada, since 1978.

The decision to document our experiences grew out of a faculty retreat two years ago, when instructors were sharing humorous anecdotes about their outreach teaching adventures. After regaling each other with stories about mice in bedrooms, noisy motels, gastronomic disasters, and being awakened in the early hours by a local hooker, not to mention problems experienced in the classroom, the discussion took a more serious turn. The best theory always grows out of practice, not the other way around, and as we continued to talk it became obvious that we had begun to identify some important educational principles.

Until recently, Canada's aboriginal people have largely been excluded from post-secondary education. Education has the potential to both liberate and oppress, and fearing assimilation "through the back door" aboriginal people have sometimes been suspicious of schooling offered by people from a different culture. At a more practical level, Native people may have had other reasons to be skeptical about education. Many have not done well in under-resourced schools in the past, while most of those who have excelled have been forced to leave their communities because of the lack of locally available employment opportunities. Education has too often either enhanced a collective sense of failure for aboriginal people, or robbed their communities of some of their strongest potential leaders.

Recently there has been a growing recognition by Native leaders of the importance of having formal educational credentials which are recognized by non-native society as well as within aboriginal communities themselves. Native people have frequently said that they don't want to be patronised or offered a "watered down" curriculum, but that they do want access to culturally relevant programs. Or as one writer so succinctly put it, they want relevance without "dilution or deletion" (Pelech).

Academic institutions for their part continue to be concerned about educational standards which, in turn, tend to reflect caucasian, middle class, urban, male, values. The question of standards has also been a concern for professional associations who have trusted social work schools to deliver competent programs and to screen out unsuitable students before they can do harm to clients. The challenge for GMCC instructors and administrators, has been to address these different perspectives; a difficult task which becomes even more challenging given funding uncertainties and the constant struggle to find suitably trained and competent adult educators from both aboriginal and non-aboriginal backgrounds.

Native students want an education which equips them to work both in their own rural communities as well as in non-native urban settings. As one writer, (Restivo), quoting a

Native Elder, put it, aboriginal learners want to be able "to walk in both worlds with one spirit."

In reviewing the chapters of this book, a number of related themes become apparent. The most successful instructors have usually been the most humble, and Paulo Freire's notions of adult education appear to have influenced a number of the writers. Freire has been most critical of more conventional teachers who function according to him as "bankers," dispensing irrefutable knowledge in a dispassionate way to uncritical consumers. Freire has suggested that this is a narrow and oppressive approach to learning, and one which fails to produce the critical thinkers which healthy communities need. Those of us who fashion our teaching after Freire or his North American counterparts, Myles Horton and Malcolm Knowles endeavour to minimize status differentials between ourselves and our students, and to engage them in a process of "authentic dialogue." This involves letting students get to know us and in the process making ourselves vulnerable, and presenting our expertise not as absolute truth, but as a wisdom which is negotiable.

It would be naive to argue that this style of teaching always works. Native people have been the victims of colonial policies for too long, and the concept of "learned helplessness" accompanied by a passive approach to learning is not unknown to them. Indeed it may be culturally sanctioned. Even so, those instructors who are committed to a reciprocal model of learning, who respect the wisdom of their students, who acknowledge cultural difference, and who are knowledgeable, trustworthy, and approachable are the ones most popular with students, and probably the most effective.

A second important theme to emerge in this book has been related to curriculum, and in particular, the emphasis which has been placed on the value of including a personal development component. Social workers have always known that they can only take the client as far as they have gone in their own personal development, and that unless the worker is emotionally healthy, they cannot help a client significantly. Social work is not merely an intellectual process. As one British social work academic put it, it is about client and worker communicating "middle to middle" (Bill Jordan). It is a collaborative activity. Native communities have experienced more than their fair share of hurt in the past. The healing process has to begin first with those who are to be the helpers of the future.

All GMCC social work courses require students to engage with the class material in a meaningful way, and to do more than merely memorize information and demonstrate technical competence. There is also the expectation that exposure to new ideas and concepts will encourage students to gain new insights into themselves and their relationships, and by so doing identify areas they need to work on more intensively outside the classroom. In the case of outreach programs, access to specialist counsellors in a rural community is usually limited, and it is partly to compensate for this that the intensive personal development opportunities are offered at the outset of each program. Where major personal issues persist, instructors will help students locate appropriate resources elsewhere and support students through any subsequent trauma which might interfere with their studies.

Related to the issue of healing has been the need to assist students to develop a strong sense of self. Many Native people have an incomplete understanding of their culture or have felt uncomfortable taking pride in their ethnic origins. The introduction of a spirituality component into the curriculum, taught by Elders as well as other knowledgeable aboriginal instructors has proven to be invaluable to the process of producing self-aware, self-assured, competent, aboriginal social workers.

Conflict is the midwife of change (Freire). Indeed, conflict and change are often inextricably linked. Consequently, the instructors, coordinators, and administrators of effective social work programs cannot always expect "smooth sailing." As students become more critically aware they frequently begin to change their behaviours, sometimes to the chagrin of their family and community members.

Social work is about change at both personal and societal levels. It is therefore by definition a political process. It involves challenging the unequal distribution of power at the individual, family, and community levels. When people who have been silenced begin to speak out for the first time, their voices are sometimes passionate, angry, and ambivalent. Sometimes an instructor can become a convenient target for years of pent-up emotion, and it is difficult at such times not to feel defensive or to resist the temptation to hurl verbal barbs back at the ungrateful learner. Although this would be an understandable response, it would also be the absolute wrong one if the goal of the instructor is to facilitate student empowerment.

From the beginning, the Social Work Program at GMCC has found that the hiring of a competent, compassionate, trustworthy, on-site coordinator has been vital to the success of its outreach programs. Not only can this person provide support to students during times of distress, he/she is also an invaluable link between the college and the community it serves, and can play a key role in reducing negative consequences associated with conflict. Coordinators therefore have to possess above average interpersonal skills and be perceived as credible professionals by all the people with whom they work.

This book is presented as an honest account of GMCC's history of teaching social work to aboriginal students. It has not been edited for political correctness. Some mistakes in delivering our outreach programs have inevitably been made, but overall we are proud of our achievements over the past fifteen or so years. We believe our success has been due not just to the efforts of instructors and administrators, but also to the willingness of students to take risks, and their families and communities to support them.

This book would not have been possible without the efforts of many people including those mentioned elsewhere on the list of contributors; GMCC President, Dr. Gerry Kelly who has encouraged our efforts all along; Dr. Paul Otke, Dean of Community Services, who gave invaluable support to the project; Jannie Edwards and members of the GMCC Faculty Development committee, who arranged for some financial support to the project; Marilyn Yaremko our patient secretary; Cathy Conroy, our intrepid editor who worked wonders with some sometimes difficult manuscripts; Kathy Alexis who provided our cover illustration; and last, but by no means least, Kevin Collard, our layout expert, who can take full credit for the way this book looks.

Kay Feehan and David Hannis,
Edmonton, Alberta, Canada
July 1993

Chapter 1

Vision and Values

Kay Feehan

It began with three dreams. These dreams existed in the souls of three different groups; they were dreams of what could be, and indeed, of what should be.

The Native leaders dreamed about restoring the pride and self-determination of their people. It was a dream of moving away from the apathy, despair, and marginalization in which many Native people lived. It was a dream of having their own indigenous social workers and community activators.

The Native people dreamed of the flowering of their individual potential. It was a dream of utilizing their inherent abilities to become helpers and healers with their own communities.

The social work educators dreamed about what their work could achieve. It was a dream of empowering Native people and enhancing their natural skills, which would enable them to achieve their aspirations.

These dreams were slowly revealed, and they eventually became one dream—a dream whose fulfillment would significantly change people and communities. This dream involved a two-way learning process in which instructors and administrators would both be touched, and learning would flow not only from instructor to student but also, in a very real way, from student to instructor. Each would be challenged and enriched by the other.

Dream fulfilment often involves hard work, pain, frustration, and experimentation, and ultimately, unbelievable satisfactions. There were achievements and there were failures, but their belief in the goal sustained the social work dreamers. Their ultimate goal was to train Native people for the social work profession and to do so in harmony with the culture and values of the aboriginal people while maintaining the integrity of the curriculum. To sustain the balance between educational standards and local needs was a continuing struggle; compromises and adjustments on both sides were required. However, an increasing number of Native graduates; their positive written and verbal evaluations; and their personal stories of growth, change, and achievement finally demonstrated the success of our work.

This chapter identifies the six themes that formed the philosophic base of Grant MacEwan Community College's (GMCC) Social Work Outreach Programs for aboriginal peoples. These themes reflected the thinking and approach of our programs from the time they began in 1978. They were the essential threads that bound our curriculum and program delivery.

In response to Native requests, the GMCC Social Work Outreach program integrated the following six themes:

- Native identity
- Self-determination
- Self awareness and personal development
- Responsibility and self-esteem
- Prevention and change (not maintenance)
- Similar academic quality

Native Identity

Social work programs have often been accused of employing a white, middle-class approach to their professional interventions with minority groups. From the beginning, it was vital to the GMCC Social Work Faculty that we avoid this pitfall and develop a culturally sensitive educational process. The first needs assessment, which was done among Native welfare workers in the Hobbema area, in 1977, identified that two of their top four concerns were maintaining a Native identity and acknowledging the social, personal, professional, and political situations on the reserves (Kuwada, 1979). We believed that it would be more effective for students to develop counselling approaches within a familiar cultural setting than it would be to expect them to adjust to some university –imposed criteria or techniques of counselling (Minor, 1981).

The challenge to incorporate Native culture and Native values into our Social Work Program has always been paramount. Although our students were of Native ancestry, in many instances, they did not understand what this ancestry meant. Some rejected their background, while others retained a dormant pride in their race, but only a few had deeply explored their cultural heritage. Historically, Native people come from different and distinct cultures and tribes. To generalize extensively about their values and life styles is inappropriate. The insights into their culture had to come from the students themselves and from the bands.

For most educators, speculation about another person's culture is patronizing, and of course, unrealistic. Culture is how we live; it is a learned, shared, changeable, diverse, and cumulative experience (Schusky & Culbert, 1978). No one can speak as an expert about another's culture. Only someone who lives the culture daily can identify what that culture means. Thus, we saw ourselves as the content experts and our Native students as the cultural experts. Through open exploration, we hoped to facilitate their encounters with social work theory so that they could adapt the ideas that best fit their experience. We tried to enhance our students' cultural and personal self-confidence so that they could choose which of our instructional tools would best contribute to their growing pride of nation. As one Native social worker in the Yukon stated in her program evaluation, "We are trying to bring back the harmony and respect of the past—It is coming" (McLaughlin, 1980).

We learned that stereotypical approaches about Native customs were dangerous but that learning about common Native beliefs from the Natives themselves was helpful. The literature on appropriate adaptations to cultural conditions was meager. However, what we learned from Native leaders and elders, and particularly from our Native students, (by attending their ceremonies, and listening to their ideas), expanded our awareness of their lifestyles immeasurably.

Incorporating Native material into our curriculum involved a combination of the following approaches:

- **Specific Native content provided by Native people.** Thus, special courses such as Selected Issues SS 403.3 focused directly on Native cultural awareness.

- **Including Native ceremonies** such as sweetgrass ceremonies and morning prayers into class time and integrating some student or Elder-identified concepts such as the significance of the circle into course content.

- **Using teaching methodologies** that emphasized experiential learning and using examples from students' personal experiences to demonstrate theory.

- **Revising all courses to reflect Native content.** This approach was consistent with suggestions of other educators such as, "There should be relevant Native content in the total curriculum not solely in courses of Native study specialization" (Collins et al., 1985).

- **Enhancing instructor sensitivity to cultural aspects.** It was important for our instructors to understand the model of the Native families, including the traditional, the transitional, and the present day family as well as the significance of the extended family.

- **Supporting traditional spirituality,** consensus problem solving, oral traditions, sharing and elder wisdom.

These curriculum modifications were confirmed by Audrey McLaughlin's recommendation that it was urgent that the Social Work Program contain an "assurance that students will not gain a professional identity at the expense of losing a cultural identity" (McLaughlin, 1980).

We received a positive response to the inclusion and integration of Native content into the GMCC Social Work Program. For example, 90% of Yukon students rated this aspect highly (McLaughlin, 1980). Although our attempts to hire Native instructors varied (from 50% in the Yukon program to 10% in other areas), there were at least some instructors of Native ancestry in every program, and a concerted effort was made to have Elders present at various times. Audrey McLaughlin stated, "Many students began to explore questions of Indian traditions and identify some for the first time and this developed a stronger sense of pride and confidence in traditional values" (McLaughlin, 1980).

Self-determination

The need for Social Work education was intertwined with the aboriginal people's articulated desire to manage their own social services. The demand for native self-government culminated in statements that were contained in the proposed 1992 Charlottetown Constitutional Accord.

Social Work Outreach programs developed because many aboriginal people wanted to shift from being passive social welfare recipients to become managers and controllers of their own social services and programs. The GMCC program at Lesser Slave Lake, for example, resulted from a 1983 "tri-partite agreement" signed by the Alberta and the Federal Governments which transferred the responsibility for delivering child welfare services to the bands. The Yellowhead Tribal Program and the High Level Regional Council Programs arose from this movement toward more Native control.

The emphasis in the GMCC Social Work curriculum was on developing Native professionals who would use the knowledge and skills they obtained to assume their cultural responsibility. They were not simply learning skills in order to maintain the "old" services or to become assistants to non-Native "bosses." Their knowledge of traditional social work theories combined with a professional vocabulary became enabling tools that allowed them to interact with other helping professionals on an equal basis.

There was, and continues to be among our faculty, a strong belief in Paulo Freire's statement "that education should liberate" (Freire, 1984).

Self awareness and personal development

As social work educators, we believe that the process of learning occurs best in an atmosphere of openness and trust. Theories become meaningful when students are able to expose themselves to a new awareness of self and have a desire to view the world in a different way. An exploration of attitudes with respect to self and others, and the formation of new concepts about self and community are the essential underpinnings to this process. Education cannot and should not be separated from the person, the job, and the community context. In that sense our program is indeed developmental (Massing, 1983).

Self-esteem and Responsibility

A major key to our success has been our program's emphasis on personal growth and healing. The negative effects that Native people experience as a result of their loss of understanding and appreciation of their Native culture are well-established. A recognition of this cultural wounding and an understanding of the aboriginal's personal journey through pain and its consequences was vital (Rodwell & Blankelday, 1992).

To teach effectively, it was first necessary to recognize that the students who were hurting and the students whose emotional energies were depleted as a result of coping with "unfinished business" could not meet the heavy program demands. Despite budget restraints and initial resistance from sponsoring groups, we insisted that an extensive personal growth component be included in our program. This component took the form of special workshops and appeared as significant sections in each course. In each program year, this specific, noncredit personal development component comprised a minimum of 100 instructional hours.

In all program evaluations, the value of the personal growth component was confirmed. One student summarized it clearly, "Personal development – the worst time but the best" (McLaughlin, 1985). Other comments, "The emphasis of self-awareness and identity in the workshops was a growth-producing experience which often led to a greater understanding of oneself and others" supported this confirmation (Kuwada, 1979).

The personal growth component did not focus exclusively on the enhancement of a student's self-image; it was partnered with the professional "use of self" concept, which is necessary in order to help others. Thus, the themes of self-esteem and responsibility are not separate but vitally connected. The concept of "person power" was identified as a tool for enhancing community power and reinforcing self-determination and Native control. The emphasis on taking responsibility seems to have a powerful influence on others in the Native community. Such a result was demonstrated when the mother of a student in our Slave Lake Program proudly proclaimed that her son was the first of the extended family to take a post-secondary education program and, she prophesied, he would encourage others to do the same. That prophesy was fulfilled in a unique way when she herself graduated from the Grouard program. "I never believed I could do it" she confided.

Prevention and Change

Special emphasis was placed on preventing problems or further breakdowns rather than simply maintaining the status quo or "band-aiding." In Canada, the history of Native-White relationships has been fraught with well-intentioned, but inadequate and fragmented, efforts to tackle symptoms not causes. Grant MacEwan Community College did not want to reinforce this approach. Too often social workers are pre-occupied with crisis intervention, rather than development, prevention, and education. We wanted to emphasize dealing with the underlying causes of problems and utilizing the strengths of the community. Our program's community practice components are somewhat unique. When examining a Band's community needs, we apply the model of the circle, which includes the economic, spiritual, recreational, educational, cultural, health, and political interactions of the community.

Affirmative action formed part of many student assignments and projects. Their activities ranged from a brief on the Old Man Dam by the Peigans, to the establishment of alcohol prevention programs in Northern Alberta, to lobbying for and developing constructive services on a variety of reserves. One community assignment saw students in High Level delivering a community-based workshop on Women's Issues. Through education, individuals change as they encounter new ideas and struggle to absorb an expanded perspective of the world. Thus, to the delight of some and the dismay of others, the students emerging from our program had, in different ways and in different areas, experienced significant attitude changes. The "ripple effect" ensured that when their attitudes changed, the impact would be felt in their families and in their communities. The awareness of this effect placed a heavy responsibility on program planners. It was a natural evolution that occurred when students responded to the instructional materials and to the best social work theories.

Our faculty respected the aboriginals' life values and wanted to build on these strengths. As McLaughlin (1985) reported, "Indian Social Services have often replicated the dysfunctional systems which Indian control has hoped to redress." Our dream was to be enablers—to provide a supportive environment in which our students would come to know the dominant culture's methods and to gain enough confidence in their own cultural approaches to select and implement the changes that would best suit their needs.

Similar Academic Quality

To believe in our students is to believe deeply in their inherent capacity for learning. There was an insidious pressure, which came under many guises, to deliver a program that was "watered-down" or substantially different from the program delivered to other students from the dominant society. Emma La Roque (1975) suggested that teachers of Natives had low student expectations; they could not trust their students to be competent on their own. We did not want to fall into this trap. We believed that it would be a mistake to expect anything less than quality standards from all our students. However, this expectation does not imply that all curriculum and methodologies must be identical. Incorporating Native cultural values into our curriculum, addressing in class the issues that arose from the rural–Native environment in which our students lived and worked called for program sensitivity and unique instructional approaches.

Achieving a balance between academic standards and the needs of special groups is a delicate task. Many checks and measures were required to produce this balance. Employing on-campus instructors who taught the same course (with cultural adaptations in the materials but not in standards) helped ensure conformity to the accreditation standards. Transferring students from an outreach situation to a traditional, on-campus program on occasion and carefully monitoring their progress, helped to guarantee that they received a similar quality of instruction. The tension that was generated while attempting to reconcile the notion of maintaining academic integrity with meeting Native community demands is an issue that writers Castellano, Stalwick, and Wien (1986) have also identified.

Our program identified and strongly supported the six themes discussed in this chapter. In implementing them we were, as always, faced with obstacles that hindered us, and occasionally we did not achieve the optimum situation. Nevertheless, those themes guided our deliberations, our negotiations, and our instructional delivery systems. How we achieved our goal is discussed in other chapters in this text.

Figure 1.1

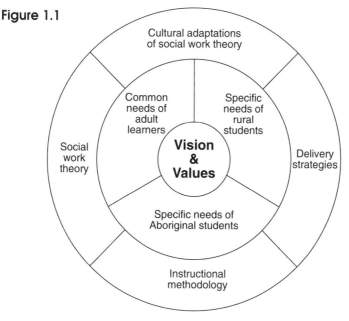

In retrospect, we chose wisely, and these core themes continue to sustain our program delivery. Because societal conditions have changed since 1978 along with various concepts in education and in aboriginal status, our content, methodologies, and delivery modes have been adjusted accordingly. However, the values and themes we identified have proven relevant and adaptable. They provided the path to our dream fulfillment. They form the core of the GMCC Social Work Program's instructional model, and are reflected in each layer of our curriculum planning process. Figure 1.1 is a graphic representation of this model.

The instructional model incorporates adult learning theory with the issues that affect rural students such as the isolated, fragmented social services available, the duplication of and gaps in services, and the inherent difficulties of working with relatives and neighbours (Feehan, 1988). These same factors are intensified in aboriginal communities. Aboriginal students must also learn to deal with Band structures and interactions as well as their relationships with the community's traditional helpers and Band administrators.

Our instructional methodologies emphasize creative and student-centered approaches to learning with minimum use of lectures and maximum student involvement in group discussions. Role-plays, case studies, personal inventories, videotaping sessions, triads, group presentations, debates and puppets are instructional techniques that have proved successful.

Our delivery strategies included the hiring of a fulltime coordinator who became the prime nurturer, and tutor for our Native students. The coordinator helped students to become accountable for their own learning and to meet program expectations with respect to attendance and assignments. The "up-front" inclusion of remedial English and non-credit personal development courses helped ensure that Native students were adequately prepared both academically and personally to undertake the rigors of the social work program. Modularizing the format of our course materials proved successful as did extending the hours for each course. Our system of closely monitoring the students, providing developmental opportunities for coordinators and instructors, and encouraging skills training for field supervisors led to some rich and powerful learning opportunities. This is not to claim that some magic educational utopia has evolved; mistakes and problems continue to challenge us.

Nevertheless it began with three dreams. The dreams of the Native leaders, the Native people and the social work educators have, to a substantial degree, been realized. They have proven to be attainable and not mere fantasies. The emotion and pride evidenced at the Native Social Work convocations is the realization of these dreams. As these graduates claim their diplomas, the Native's dream of becoming helpers and healers in their own communities, and the social work educators dream of empowering their Native students to achieve their aspirations are all fulfilled in a satisfying and significant way.

References

Berger, R. (1992). Student Retention: A critical phase in the academic careers of minority baccalaureate social workers. *Journal of Social Work Education,* 28(1), 85–96.

Castellano, M. B., Stalwick, H., & Wien, F. (1986). Native Social Work Education in Canada Issues and Adaptations. *Canadian Social Work Review,* 167–183.

Collins, D., Reichwein B., & Westwood, R. (1985). *Training of Rural and Native People for Work in Social Services.* A discussion paper, Alberta Advanced Education.

Feehan, K. (1988). *Faculty Resource Book – Readings on Native & Rural Social Work.* Edmonton, AB: Grant MacEwan Community College.

Freire, P. (1984). *Pedagogy of the Oppressed.* New York Continuum.

Kuwada, T. (1979). Final Report, Native Social Service Worker Program.

Lane, P. (1984). *The sacred tree.* (Four Winds Project). Lethbridge, AB: University of Lethbridge Press, 74–82.

LaRoque, E. (1975). *Defeathering the Indian.* Agincourt, ON: Book Society of Canada Ltd.

Malaspina College Students (1980). *The Teaching of the Elders*. National Health & Welfare, Medical Services Branch.

Massing, D. (1983). *Proposal for Outreach Delivery*. Edmonton, AB: Grant MacEwan Community College.

McLaughlin, A. (1980). *Evaluation Native Social Services Worker Program Yukon*. Edmonton, AB: Grant MacEwan Community College.

McLaughlin, A. (1984). *Evaluation Native Social Service Workers Outreach*. Slave Lake, AB.

McLaughlin, A. (1985). *Interim Report Native Social Services Worker Program*. Blue Quills, AB.

McLaughlin, A. (1986). *Evaluation Social Services Worker Program*. Blue Quills, AB.

McLaughlin, A. (1987). *Evaluation Social Services Worker Program*. Blue Quills, AB.

Minor, N. K. M. (1981). *Counselling Among Cultures*. Unpublished manuscript.

Nakarieski, Manuel, Rittner, B. (1992). The Inclusionary Cultural Model. *Journal of Social Work Education,* 28(1), 27–34.

Northwest Indian Child Welfare Institute (no date). *Hertigate and Helping: A Model Curriculum for Indian Child Welfare Practice*. Portland, OR.

Pace, J., & Smith, F.V. (1990). Native social work education. *Canadian Social Work Review,* 7(1), 109–118.

Rodwell, M. K., & Blankebaker, A. (1992). Strategies for Developing Cross-Cultural Sensitivity – Wounding as Metaphor. *Journal of Social Work Education,* 28(2), 163–164.

Schusky, E.L. & Culbert, T.P. (1973). *Introducing Culture* (3rd ed.). Englewood Cliff, NJ: Prentice-Hall.

Tobin, M. (1992). *Northern Perspectives: Practice & Education in Social Work Education*. Winnipeg, MN: Manitoba Association of Social Workers & University of Manitoba.

Chapter 2

Cherishing the Sacred

Kay Feehan

In developing delivery strategies for Grant MacEwan Community College's (GMCC) Social Work Program for Aboriginal Peoples many educational issues, beyond the usual adult learner's models, were considered. In addition to attending to cultural approaches, the following issues were examined:

- the impact on the extended family and the community;
- our students' sense of responsibility for their families;
- the emphasis on spiritual values;
- the differences in nonverbal communication;
- the importance of mutual respect between students and instructors;
- the use of visual learning, and
- the need to demonstrate, not just talk about, concepts.

In this chapter, I would like to examine two of these issues and demonstrate how they enriched our instructional process. A good educational "stew" requires two basic ingredients: sound theory, and caring, competent instructors. In our program, the seasoning came from cultural sensitivity and flexibility.

Cherishing the Sacred

We began with the emphasis on spiritual values. In mainstream education, there appears to be a resistance to discussing the spiritual. The North American concept of separation of Church and State has led to a fear of exploring not only denominational religion but also the whole concept of spirituality. Our Western culture is becoming increasingly scientific and relativistic, and former values appear to some moderns to be anachronistic. Thus, contradictions, disintegration, and rejection of value orientations with respect to the spiritual are common. Humanistic psychologists such as Carl Rogers, Rollo May, Viktor Frankl, and Erick Fromm take a philosophical approach to what it means to be fully human and to questions regarding one's purpose in life and the meaning of existence. Other theorists, especially those with behaviouristic orientations, downplay concepts that relate to the sacred.

Currently, the American Council on Social Work Education is revising its accreditation standards to re-instate references to spirituality as a valid topic for social work educators. Such topics were prevalent in the early 1970's, but later, all mention of spirituality as valuable content was deleted. This type of reversal is indicative of the confusion surrounding the relevancy of spirituality in social work practice.

One of the many gifts that aboriginal students have given their instructors and program administrators is their deep sense of the spiritual. Their simple, natural respect for the Great Spirit and their own inner spirit has helped to inspire and sustain these students. The stories of the Elders and the behavior of many Native people reflect instructions such as "Each morning upon rising, and each evening before sleeping, give thanks for the life within you and for all life, for the good things the Creator has given you." (Lane, 1984) Such rituals have formed a vital part of our students' daily experience.

In attempting to understand Native culture, Western instructors must recognize the spiritual significance of the many concepts and beliefs they will encounter in the teaching process. A few social work theorists have discussed the importance of religion in understanding the client system, and Pinderhughes (1989) and O'Brien (1992) have cited the importance of recognizing religion as a means of understanding ethnicity. Many social work educators, however, ignore the spiritual aspect and remove themselves from the experiences of their students. Yet, it should be obvious that, given the primacy of spirituality in aboriginal people's lives, educators must be cognizant of the spiritual needs of their students and their students' families and be familiar with the resources and spiritual practices that can provide an important source of social support (Sullivan, 1992). For example, in the education of aboriginal students, the concept of the Circle is held Sacred because the Great Spirit causes everything in Nature to be round. Many aboriginal practices incorporate the symbolism of the circle, and instructors can integrate this concept in simple ways such as circular classroom seating arrangements.

This relationship between everyday life and the spiritual is reinforced in many of the educational resources that Natives themselves have assembled. "Indian child welfare training functions with a value for... the various spiritual beliefs held among Indian people." (Northwest Indian Child Welfare Institute, 1984)

One Elder, Eddie Bellrose, identified the following as a graphic model of understanding the person:

More aboriginal people acknowledge the indivisible connection of these three elements than many in our dominant white society. One of our students (Stebbins, 1988) expressed it this way: "The beliefs, spirituality, and culture is what makes a person's solidity as a freely functioning human being." She suggested that the absence of the spiritual dimension represented a serious lack. Good social work teachers, who emphasize person-centered therapies, should be able to incorporate into the classroom the essence of the spiritual dimension. Knowing and respecting the students' spiritual traditions and practices affirms their dignity and worth and sheds significant light on their underlying personal issues and their potential coping skills (Sheridan et al., 1992). People who have struggled with long-term mental illness or who have recovered from addictive afflictions believe that one of the major shortcomings of the therapeutic community is its avoidance of spirituality (Simons 1992).

Social workers affirm that they build on strengths, and one of the strengths of traditional Native culture is its sustaining trust in the Creator. It has been demonstrated that the treatment of addiction, in all cultural groups, is more successful when spiritual elements are incorporated with the therapy. This combination has been particularly significant in the addictions work being done by Native groups such as the Nechi Institute in Edmonton. Native religious practices are now being encouraged in Alberta correctional institutions, and in Saskatchewan a Native healing lodge is being built for women convicts.

In order to successfully integrate spirituality with teaching, instructors must first assess their deepest personal beliefs. Without this introspection and reflection on one's personal spiritual journey, one can achieve only a superficial acknowledgement of another person's beliefs.

In the practice of social work, professional helpers continually attempt to touch others in ways that help and heal them. Their desire is to facilitate the development of authentic and fully functioning persons. Maslow's self-actualization theory includes a hierarchy of needs that pertain to truth, goodness, and beauty. These needs are spiritual needs, and they are rooted in man's desire to be in harmony with the Highest Good – or Great Spirit (Maslow, 1968). Thus, social workers help others to fulfill their spiritual needs, and thus, strengthen both the individual and the community. The existential thinkers suggested that self-actualization cannot be attained if it becomes an end in itself, but rather it should be considered only a side effect of self-transcendence (Frankl 1971).

Aboriginal people are strongly grounded in the sense and awe of the spiritual. Sometimes this predisposition has clashed with the dominant culture, and through the process of colonization, a paradox was created. It involved negating Native spiritual beliefs by denying their existence, and at the same time, imposing Western religion as if the concept of religion had not previously existed among Natives. This whole scale religious imposition did not allow for an integration of new forms of worship, which would have blended both Aboriginal and Western rituals.

The man who sat on the ground in his tipi meditating on life and its meaning, accepting the kinship of all creatures and acknowledging unity with the universe of things was infusing into his being the true essence of civilization. And when Native man left off this form of development, his humanization was retarded in growth.

Chief Luther Standing Bear

Many aboriginal people are now rediscovering and revaluing their unique spirituality as Native people, and this process should be incorporated into a holistic approach to Native personal development and the social work interventions practised in their communities. The existential concepts that deal philosophically with the meaning of life have a special application for Native people, and they are more attuned to their natures than cognitive theories such as Reality, Rational Emotive, or Behaviour Therapies.

As an instructor and an administrator, some of my most cherished moments came from sharing my students' tributes to the Great Spirit and participating in traditional rituals such as the Sweet Grass ceremonies. During the Yukon program orientation, one of the first questions I was asked was if our college system allowed students to begin their day with a prayer. This spiritual beginning to the day helped students put a perspective on their studies that promoted a sense of self-worth and dignity, which in turn affected their approach to the helping profession. The classroom was now transformed into a place where special learning occurred. One of my more poignant memories of these classes occurred during the Sacred Circle, with everyone holding hands and one student thanking the Spirit for the learning. This simple prayer, a blend of Native and Christian religion, always produced a stirring moment and I experienced a deep inner peace.

Another treasured moment was one I shared with my High Level tribal students. It occurred after a smudging. We sat together in our circle, listened to a student offer a prayer, and then having created an atmosphere of trust, we all expressed our honest feelings about the progress of the program. It was an evaluation with a twist, but one I believe was extremely effective.

My most unforgettable experience occurred with our students in Slave Lake. At the end of a day of hard work and holistic learning, Dr. Pam Colorado led us through a moving Sweetgrass ceremony. Students, instructors, and administrators gathered outside around an open and "clean" fire. Yellow leaves floated down upon us and the warmth of a gorgeous fall day embraced our souls as well as our bodies. The non-Native participants gained an intuitive appreciation of the interconnectedness of Nature—between Mother Earth and the Great Spirit. All three of these experiences remind me of the words of Carl G. Jung (1983) who said, "Learn your theories as well as you can, but put them aside when you touch the miracle of the living soul."

Every outreach program had its own spiritual practices. They were initiated by the students, and they reflected their values, their orientation. Instructors facilitated these opportunities but remained non-directive. This formal acknowledgement of the value of the spiritual in learning has added a unique dimension to our outreach aboriginal programs.

Cherishing the Family Bonds

The second important element we incorporated into our programs was a sensitivity to the impact these courses would have on the extended family and the community of every aboriginal student. The Indian community is a network with many complex inter-relationships. The members have multiple roles: friend, neighbour, relative, community service volunteer, job-related service giver, and service receiver. The community is the dominant system, and the families are its subsystems. In the tribal community, people are interdependent, and normally it is through these natural networks that people seek out and receive help. The connectedness of these individuals can again be expressed through the following illustration:

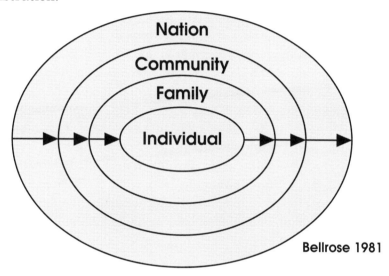

Bellrose 1981

Understanding the impact of our program on the extended family was important for several reasons. First, we had to consider the effect of the program on the students themselves, and second we had to accommodate the Native family's concerns with respect to issues involving child welfare and other social work interventions.

As members of an interdependent network, our students often felt responsible for their extended families, and much of their energy was spent attending to family responsibilities. The act of balancing College and family life poses a challenge for any student, but for Native students the challenge is even greater. Our students were often primary care-givers to a variety of family members, and in many cases, they were the motivators and strength of the family. Because these students were usually the first ones in their families to receive a post-secondary education, they became both the elect and the envied of the community. There are few student role models and fewer student family support role models for them to follow. Their family members continued to expect to receive their customary attention. The tradition of welcoming any family members who chose to come to live with them often created a conflict for the students. The responsibility of extending hospitality and the responsibility of completing assignments may seem to be incompatible.

One method of helping our students cope with these dilemmas came from Ann Manyfingers, Native Children's Advocate, Alberta Department of Social Services. She encourages students to follow the "concept of a greater good." This concept helps students to recognize that their academic priorities should come first. They come to appreciate that a greater good will ultimately benefit their families and communities if they devote their current time to learning skills.

For social work educators working in Native cultures where kinship ties are extremely important, the impact of the program on the extended family becomes significant (Pincus & Minahan, 1973). Social work techniques that ignore the value of the extended family network will not only be ineffective and inappropriate, they may also be counterproductive and even destructive. Unlike the dominant white society's concept of family, the term family, in the aboriginal sense, refers to the entire extended community network.

Three elements characterize a family: the decision-making process; life-cycle transition points; and shared rituals (Carter and McGoldrick, 1989). These elements will differ in various ethnic groups, and social work educators must be sensitized to this range of values and focus on the uniqueness of the family group. In aboriginal families, it is sometimes difficult to discern the interplay of the traditional family systems, the adaptive systems (which develop from contact with the dominant society), and the naturally evolving systems which are present in every culture. When teaching social work practice, the continuum of each of these family systems must be addressed. The best way to help Native students understand how these three elements of family apply to their culture is to draw on their personal experiences and allow them to reflect upon these experiences during a discussion of family systems.

Decision-making Processes

Students are asked to explore the decision-making processes that occur in their families of origin and families of creation. They discuss how these processes help or hinder family functioning. Aboriginal family decision-making involves the participation of a variety of extended family members, including kin who are involved by custom with that family. Often, the traditional Native consensus model is used to varying degrees, depending on the family's adherence to tradition.

Life-cycle Transition Points

Life-cycle transition points refer to the expansion, contraction, and realignment of the relationship system to support the entry, exit, and development of family members (Carter & McGoldrick, 1989). However, unique strengths in the history of aboriginal families have bestowed a richness to their life cycle whereby the whole community is involved in an individual's growth and development. Thus, the more rigid categories of the nuclear family transition points do not apply. The family boundaries are more flexible and interdependence is a norm. Today, some adaptation is being made to modern life. Certain changes have altered the former transition points, particularly with respect to the movement of young people to different homes, which are often away from the reserve and in the cities. To help aboriginals handle this shift, educators must recognize this unique aboriginal situation. They must encourage students to build on group strengths and to develop relevant and realistic strategies to help them cope with the impact this transition will have on their families. The answers must come from the student group, and the ideal instructor acts only as the facilitator.

Shared Rituals

In all families, shared rituals are crucial to the formation of identity, to bonding, and to the smooth and positive functioning of the group. Every family and every culture can identify special rituals that are unique to them. Cherishing our students' family ties enables them to name and claim these rituals. Eventually, they themselves will choose which rituals to continue, adapt, or reject.

Many aboriginal people have retained their rites of passage and ritual ceremonies. In some instances, rituals like the naming ceremony have been supplanted by or integrated with Christian baptismal ceremonies. This ritual begins the nurturing process, which may have included cradleboards, and includes moral development, nonphysical discipline, and teaching through story-telling (Northwest Indian Child Welfare Institute, 1986). Smudging, sweat lodges, pow-wows, and tea-dances are all shared rituals. Social work educators must acknowledge the significance of these rites in their classes. Like all students, aboriginal students must learn to appreciate that these existing rituals are part of a natural evolutionary process. For example, the symbolic value of the funeral and its impact on the whole community must be acknowledged both in the course content and in the attendance rules.

The roles of certain family subsystems must also be acknowledged: the elders, who are the keepers and teachers of Indian tradition; the grandparents, who are the customary teachers because of their experiences; and the children, who are particularly cherished because they represent the future of the Indian people (National Native Association of Treatment Directors, 1986).

Our program has instigated several practical means of acknowledging the extended family and recognizing that more than individual learning is at stake. One effective and popular teaching methodology is the use of genograms to illustrate family relationships. We have also incorporated activities such as the Family Day. On this day, the Yellowhead Tribal Council students bring their children, spouses, parents, or other significant family members to class. This event gives everyone a feeling of partnership in the education process. In the Yukon program, and again at Blue Quills, a new born infant attended class each day with its mother. This situation is natural for aboriginal students, and perhaps it best represents the unique adaptations that are being made to Social Work Outreach programs. The richness of our course content is continually enhanced as aboriginal students contribute their unique perspectives. Their contributions have convinced us that we must continue to cherish the sacred and the family bonds.

References

Bellrose, E. (1981). Workshop Presentation *Native Cultural Approaches* for Social Work Faculty. Edmonton, AB: GMCC.

Carter, B. & McGoldrick, M. (1989). *The changing life cycle.* Needhan Heights, MA: Allyn & Bacon.

Davis, L. E. (1984). *Ethnicity in social group work practice.* New York: Haworth Press.

Elliott, J. L. (1983). *Two nations, many cultures.* Englewood Cliffs, NJ: Prentice-Hall.

Feehan, K. (1983). *Theories of Counselling for Outreach Delivery.* Edmonton, AB: GMCC.

Frankl, V. E. (1971). *Man's search for meaning.* New York: Washington Square Press.

Green, J. W. (1982). *Cultural awareness in the human services. Englewood Cliffs, NJ: Prentice-Hall.*

Johnson, P. (1983). *Native children and the child welfare system.* Toronto, ON: Canadian Council on Social Development.

Jung, C. (1983). *The essential Jung.* Princeton, NJ: Princeton University Press.

Lane, P. (1984). *The sacred tree.* (Four Winds Project). Lethbridge, AB: University of Lethbridge Press.

Martens, T., Daily, B., & Hodgson, M. (1988). *The spirit weeps.* Edmonton, AB: Nechi Institute Publications.

Maslow, A. (1968). *Toward a psychology of being.* New York: Van Nostrand Reinhardt.

McGoldrick, M., Pearce, J. K., & Giordano, J. (1982). *Ethnicity & family therapy.* New York: Guilford Press.

Morales, A. (1983). *Social work: A profession of many faces* (3rd ed.). Boston, MA: Allyn & Bacon.

National Native Association of Treatment Directors. (1989). *In the spirit of the family.* Calgary, AB.

Northwest Indian Child Welfare Institute. (1984). *Training issues and methods in Indian Child Welfare.* Portland, OR.

Northwest Indian Child Welfare Institute. (1986). *Positive Indian parenting.* Portland, OR.

O'Brien, P. (July, 1992). *Improving the human condition.* Paper presented at the I.F.S.W. World Assembly, Washington, D.C.

Pincus, A., & Minahan, A. (1973). *Social work practice: Model and method.* Itasca, IL: Peacock Publishers.

Pinderhughes, E. (1989). *Understanding race, ethnicity and power.* New York: New York Free Press.

Richardson, R. (1991). *Family ties that bind.* Vancouver, BC: International Self-Counsel Press.

Rogers, C. (1983). *Freedom to Learn for the 80's.* Columbus, OH: Charles E. Merrill Pub. Co.

Sheridan, M. J., Ballis, R., Adcock, C. R., Berlin, S. D., & Miller, P. C. (1992). Practitioners' personal & professional attitudes and behaviors toward religion and spirituality: Issues for education and practice. *Journal of Social Work Education, 28*(2), 190–206.

Simons, B. (1992). Acknowledging spirituality in recovery: A mental health consumer's perspective. *Spirituality & Social Work Journal, 3*(1), 5–7.

Stebbins, E. (1988). *A theory as to why the emotional breakdown of the Native being.* Unpublished manuscript. Edmonton, AB: GMCC, Social Work Program.

Sullivan, W. P. (1992). Spirituality as social support for individuals with severe mental illness. *Spirituality and Social Work Journal, 3*(1), 7–13.

Westermeyer, J. (1980). *Erosion of Indian mental health in cities.* Minneapolis, MN: Department of Psychiatry, University of Minnesota.

Wilkinson, G. T. (1980, October). On assisting Indian people. *Social Casework. 61*(8), 451–454.

Chapter 3

Who is the Client?

Contracts and social work outreach programs in Native communities

Michael Kim Zapf

Who is the client? What are we trying to accomplish? What can we expect of each other in our work together? Most models of social work practice attach great importance to the tasks of clearly identifying the client and developing a working contract. It has been argued that such clarity and commitment to specific measurable goals is precisely what distinguishes the professional social worker from the do-gooder or the volunteer helper. A recent debate in the literature pushes the issue even further by proposing a covenant model to replace the narrow contract approach. Given that social work instructors often serve as role models for their students, it is ironic that social work education has been content to assume a simple contract between the institution and the student. Through my teaching experiences in Native outreach programs, I have encountered additional complex considerations that affect the working agreement between the social work student and the instructor. This chapter explores those complexities and their implications for Native outreach social work education.

In this chapter, I have deliberately chosen to use the word "credential" rather than "diploma" or "degree." The observations and arguments are based on my experiences teaching outreach courses at both the community college level (Grant MacEwan Community College, Social Work Outreach Program in High Level, Alberta) and the university level (The University of Calgary, Faculty of Social Work Aboriginal BSW Program in Spruce Grove, Alberta). I discovered that the issues with respect to contracting and instructor expectations to be similar in both settings. This book provides a rare opportunity to reflect on those experiences and to begin to develop a knowledge base that could benefit Native outreach social work education at all levels.

Contracting and Client Definition in Social Work

Determining "who is the client" has been the active starting point for models of social work practice for three decades. Perlman (1962) was one of the first to distinguish between the "applicant," who is exploring the need for service, and the "client," who has a contractual agreement with a social worker to resolve an identified problem. Subsequent writing has reinforced the notion that a social worker cannot have a client without also having a contract; by definition, a client is a person or group who has an explicit working agreement with the social worker concerning the focus of the problem and the intervention plan (Pincus & Minahan, 1973; McMahon, 1990; Zastrow, 1989; Compton & Galaway, 1989).

The following essential elements of a worker/client contract have been identified by Hudson (1989), Hepworth & Larsen (1990), and Shulman (1992):

- a statement or ranking of the goals to be accomplished (specific and observable, if possible);
- the intervention or techniques that will be used to achieve the stated goals;
- the specific roles and responsibilities of both the client and the worker;

- housekeeping and administrative items such as the duration, frequency, and location of sessions; fees; procedures for missed sessions; and overall time frame and start dates;
- provisions for reviewing, updating, and renegotiating the contract as the situation changes;
- a means of monitoring or evaluating progress towards the goals.

Such a contract ensures a "reciprocal accountability" for all phases of the work (Germain & Gitterman, 1980, p. 53), and "provides the frame of reference for the work that follows, and for understanding when the work is in process, when it is being evaded, and when it is finished" (Schwartz, 1971, p. 8).

Contracts in Social Work Education

In most urban-based social work programs, a simple contract exists between the institution and the student who is accepted into the program. The student registers and pays a fee; the school agrees to provide a specific series of courses and resources that lead to the achievement of the desired credential. While the school provides students with the opportunity to obtain the credential, each student is responsible for his or her personal engagement in the learning process. Failure to complete course requirements usually results in a failing grade; subsequent options are to repeat the course or withdraw from the program.

Instructor/Student Contract. Observing that social work instructors may act as models for their students, some writers emphasize the importance of contracting between students and instructors (Shulman, 1987; Fox & Zischka, 1989). The Course Outline can be regarded as a form of instructor/student contract, which includes the same features as a worker/client contract. The course goals are clearly stated. Class dates, locations, and instructional techniques are specified. Assignments and grading practices are made explicit.

Instructor/School Contract. On another level, instructors have a contract with the educational institution. The school agrees to certain financial compensation and provides the teaching resources and classrooms; the instructor commits to the preparation, delivery, and grading of material related to a particular course. The instructor also agrees to abide by the policies of the school, which include its grading standards. The instructor is accountable for maintaining the institution's standards in the delivery of any given course.

Instructor/Profession Contract. Related to the issue of standards, although much more ambiguous, is the instructor's contract with the profession. As members of a profession, social work faculty are not only bound to a code of professional ethics, they are also in the difficult and ill-defined position of acting as gatekeepers to screen out unsuitable students. Essentially, they perform a quality control function; they allow into the profession only those students who have proven their abilities as competent social workers (Moore & Urwin, 1990).

Contracts in Native Outreach Programs

In Native outreach programs, all three levels of contract are affected by the addition of a third party to the contract negotiations. In effect, there is another client. Frequently, a local organization (Tribal Council, Regional Council, or government department) contracts with an institution to offer the social work program, on a one-time basis, to a particular cohort of students in their constituency. Typically, the potential students are active community resource persons who work within the local social service network, either formally employed or as informal caregivers. In this situation, the community is purchasing a program to upgrade their current workers and to provide a trained resource pool for the future. The community and the school administrators negotiate a contract for the sale and purchase of a packaged social work program.

Obviously, a local organization cannot simply "purchase" the social work credential for their constituents. What the institution is selling is an opportunity, not a credential. Instructors must still assess student ability and apply the standards that maintain the integrity of the credential and the profession. Because the community is involved as a client, however, complications arise in the instructor/student, instructor/school, and instructor/profession contracts in the Native outreach context.

Instructor/Student Contract. In most urban, campus-based programs, social work instructors prepare a Course Outline that is first approved and then distributed during the first class. According to Fox & Zischka (1989), in this model

> the learning activity is structured by the teacher and the institution. The learner is told what objectives he or she is to achieve, what resources are to be used, how (and when) to use them, and how the accomplishment of the objectives will be evaluated. This imposed structure can conflict with the adult's psychological need to be self-directing and may induce resistance, apathy, or withdrawal. (p. 105)

Social work programs differ from many other academic disciplines in that the course materials are context sensitive. Because the focus of social work is on the person-environment interaction, the environment becomes a crucial factor. Algebra can be algebra anywhere; physics is physics anywhere. Effective social work practice, however, changes to acommo-date different settings. Urban-based instructors should have enough familiarity with the social problems, issues, and resources in their cities to design appropriate courses for students who will participate in classes and field placements in these urban settings. However, an instructor who is contracted to deliver a course in a Native outreach program cannot simply transfer that same course to the outreach setting. He or she must first spend time with the students and community resource persons to develop an approach to the material that reflects local issues and learning styles. Native outreach program course outlines tend to be true working contracts in the sense that they represent an ongoing negotiated agreement between the instructor and the students, with additional input provided by the community group who purchased the program.

Ricks (1991) observed that many Native northerners who want to be social workers have themselves been victimized and require healing. Often, the community cannot wait for their workers' healing processes to be complete before their services must be provided. The same observation can be made for Native outreach programs in social work education. While some personal development has preceded the social work courses, many students come to class in various stages of awareness and healing. Issues such as addictions, family violence, sexual abuse, and child welfare are not simply abstract course content areas; many of the students are, or have been, victims of these experiences. Because of the limited resources available in the community for referral, the course instructor could well be the only resource person with any expertise, and the classroom may be the only available forum for disclosure, sharing, and support related to these issues. The instructor may be required to act as counsellor and groupworker to an extent far beyond that expected of faculty in urban campus-based programs.

Instructor/School Contract. In conventional campus-based social work education programs, the instructor agrees to apply the institution's standards through specific grading practices, and thereby maintain the integrity of the credential. A student who fails a course has the option of repeating. This particular application of standards can be troublesome in outreach programs where the community is also a client. It has already been noted that the community can purchase only the opportunity, not the credential, for their students. Yet these communities commit substantial resources toward establishing a local cohort social work program. They may exert "fierce claims of ownership" (Ryan, 1987, p. 72) and have strong expectations about the learning opportunities the institution will make locally available. In a sequenced program, a failing grade in a prerequisite course can prevent a student from continuing on to other required courses. For outreach students, one failed core course can bump them out of the entire program.

Consider a situation where the student is a child welfare worker for the local Band, and he or she fails a first-year course that is a prerequisite for key courses offered in second year. Effectively, that student could be out of the social work program, unable to proceed in good standing, with no opportunity to take the course over again. Considering that this person is likely to continue doing child welfare work in the community for the next 20 years, should he or she be failed and the academic standards of the credential maintained, or should he or she be allowed to continue to have access to the courses now being offered in the local community? Should this worker have the benefit of receiving as much training as possible while it is available, or should he or she be dropped for failing to meet a certain standard of the institution? From whose perspective should these decisions be made?

Instructor/Profession Contract. The instructor's role as a gatekeeper for the profession is also complicated in Native outreach programs. Peterman & Blake (1986) identified four criteria on which schools of social work should screen out unsuitable students: grades, poor communication skills, inappropriate affect, and poor field performance. Difficulties with the relative aspects of grading have already been discussed. The remaining criteria are so culture-bound that it is not clear how an outreach instructor can make valid assessments. How can an instructor assess someone's communication skills in a language, culture, and context that is unfamiliar to the instructor? Against whose standards will field performance be assessed? How does an instructor assess appropriate affect in an unfamiliar culture where the instructor may not understand the obvious verbal and non-verbal cues let alone the deeper cultural and historic patterns to which the community members may be reacting? Can a non-Native instructor from outside the community presume to assess the "appropriate" response for people who must deal with colonialism, addictions, and systematic devaluation?

In their plea for quality control in social work education, Moore and Urwin (1990) contend that some students "require either postponement of their education goals or redirection"; they suggest that instructors provide such students "with other options such as transferring credits into another major or degree" (p. 123). Are either of these options realistic for Native outreach students? How can students postpone their education when the one-shot cohort program may be their only chance to take these courses locally? How can students be redirected to other majors that are simply not available?

Gatekeeping, or preventing inappropriate students from entering the social work profession, is not a simple task in Native outreach programs. Most of these students are more motivated by a desire to understand the forces that affect their communities and to learn skills that can help their people than by a desire to enter the profession of social work. Professional status may be a foreign concept in this setting. The application of culture-bound standards to screen out those who are perceived as unsuitable or unworthy to enter the profession ignores the community context of practice and could be regarded as a further extension of colonialism.

Covenants: An Alternative to Contracts

A recent debate in the social work literature has its roots in medical ethics. Like the worker/client relationship in social work, medicine's conventional view of the doctor/patient relationship has been based on a contract model. May (1977, 1983) criticized this approach as "minimalist" because doctors tended to provide only those services clearly spelled out in the contract. Contracts encouraged doctors to be "calculating" and "lacking in spontaneity" and perhaps not fully available to their troubled patients. As an alternative, May advocated a covenant model based on companionship, caring, commitment, and teaching.

Miller (1990) attempted to apply the covenant model to social work practice. She began with the following concerns about the limitations of social work contracts:

> Contracting not only encourages but to some degree
> requires a narrowing of focus to specific and concrete

behaviours. . . The contracting process may thus promote, at least indirectly, a minimalist social work role with clients, that is, the tendency to work only with those behaviours that can be put in a contract format. (p. 122)

Miller advocates that the covenant is a more useful model for the worker/client relationship because of its emphasis on

the inclusive and "gift" aspects of professional identity. The *inclusive* aspect means that the professional is not limited by a narrow definition of the client's problem but is committed to staying with the client throughout the client's journey in working through his or her troubles.

The key element of the covenant relationship is the professional's promise to be faithful to the gift that has been given to him or her in becoming a professional by giving it to the client and community. (p. 123)

She argues that professional social workers have received a "gift" from the community in the form of an accessible professional education, professional status, and the opportunity to continue learning from clients. These social workers make a commitment to a code of ethics and have a responsibility to return their gift to the community in the form of teaching, healing, and empowerment. She concludes by asking social workers "to view social work as a covenant to clients and the community rather than as a contract to be expeditiously completed" (p. 124).

Perhaps a covenant model can offer a new perspective on the connections between instructors, students, and the community in Native outreach social work education programs. The word "covenant" could be an unfortunate choice because its religious overtones may suggest the missionary/colonial patterns that have been so destructive for many Native communities. Once past the word, however, the covenant framework suggests a commitment that goes beyond the typical Course Outline. The instructor would commit to "staying with" the students through the contracted period of the educational program, not only as their teacher but also as their companion and counsellor. While enjoying the status, creative freedom, and other benefits of a faculty position, the instructor is responsible for returning these gifts to the community by offering students the resources and help they need to successfully complete the program.

When I was teaching a methods course in High Level, I discovered that the local language had no term for the word "contract." My notion of placing goals and roles into some sort of formal agreement was an unfamiliar concept that did not fit easily within the local community. Yet their language did include words for "responsibility" and "commitment." Perhaps the concepts inherent in the covenant model would have more meaning in Native communities.

I have referred to this discussion of the covenant model as a debate. Not everyone is enthusiastic about covenants in social work practice. Corcoran (1991) denounced the covenant model as a well-intentioned but idealized promise that leaves the client and the community "unprotected from failure to provide services" (p. 183) and "without recourse or remedy" (p. 184). Although social workers may mean well, the promises they make within a covenant are not enforceable. Comparing covenants and contracts from a legal perspective, Corcoran concludes that "only a contract ensures the promisee that the promisor will fulfil this commitment" (p. 184). When applied to the context of Native outreach education, this argument implies that a contract would protect the students by making the instructor accountable for specific content and learning opportunities. A covenant, in itself, is not sufficient here. While the students may need a committed companion and counsellor, they must also have a teacher who is able to adapt and deliver the same core material that comprises the urban campus-based program. A high graduation rate means little if the Native program is perceived to be a watered-down or second-class version.

The structure of many outreach social work programs in Native communities reveals an attempt to achieve a useful contract/covenant balance. Usually a permanent, local on-site coordinator is appointed to be with the students throughout their program and to provide necessary counselling and support functions. Individual sessional instructors then move in and out of the program with their course outline contracts.

Conclusion

We are still only beginning to develop a knowledge base for Native outreach programs in social work education. We know that things are different out there and that course content and delivery processes must be adapted, but we do not yet have clear guidelines for those tasks. This book represents an important effort to learn from the direct experiences of those who have been involved with such outreach programs in northern Alberta. As part of that effort, this chapter focuses specifically on contracts between the instructor and the students, the institutions, and the social work profession. Although we do not yet know enough to advance prescriptions for these contracts, we can say that the simple contracts of the urban, campus-based social work programs are not sufficient for Native outreach programs where the community is also an active client.

Some might argue that the proposals made in this discussion of Native outreach programs move far beyond the conventional concept of instructor to a point where the roles of teacher and social worker become confused and blurred. Yet such blurring could well be the future direction of the social work profession. The distinguished social work educator Sophie Freud has described education as a social work method, and further suggested that community education could become the "integrative framework" or the "unifying purpose" for the profession. From her perspective, direct service or clinical practice could be regarded as "educating our clients," while community work would be "educating organizations and the community on behalf of our clients' needs" (1987, p. 114).

In a previous article (Zapf, 1992), I discussed the stresses reported by social workers who work in remote communities. I described the uncomfortable fit between the profession's urban-based practice models and the needs of most northern communities. Isolated workers experience stress when they realize that the approach of the job is incompatible with active membership in the community. My recent experiences with social work outreach education in Native communities suggest that instructors in those programs encounter similar stress. The Native community actively participates in the educational process. They are active clients who dramatically affect the nature of the instructor's contracts with the students, the school, and the profession.

References

Compton, B.R., & Galaway, B. (1989). *Social work processes (4th edition)*. Belmont: Wadsworth.

Corcoran, K.J. (1991). In defense of contracts and the caveats of covenants. *Social Work, 36*(2), 183–184.

Fox, R., & Zischka, P.C. (1989). The field instruction contract: A paradigm for effective learning. *Journal of Teaching in Social Work, 3*(1), 103–116.

Freud, Sophie. (1987). Social workers as community educators: A new identity for the profession. *Journal of Teaching in Social Work, 1*(1), 111–126.

Germain, C.B., & Gitterman, A. (1980). *The life model of social work practice.* New York: Columbia.

Hepworth, D.H., & Larsen, J.A. (1990). *Direct social work practice: Theory and skills (3rd edition)*. Belmont: Wadsworth.

Hudson, J. (1989). Ingredients of a contract. In B.R. Compton & B. Galaway (Eds.) *Social work processes (4th edition)*. Belmont: Wadsworth.

May, W. (1977). Code and covenant or philanthropy and contract? In S.J. Reiser (Ed.), *Ethics in medicine: Historical perspectives and contemporary concerns.* Cambridge: MIT Press.

May, W. (1983). *The physician's covenant: Images of the healer in medical ethics.* Philadelphia: Westminster Press.

Miller, P. (1990). Covenant model for professional relationships: An alternative to the contract model. *Social Work, 35,* 121–125.

Moore, L.S., & Urwin, C.A. (1990). Quality control in social work: The gatekeeping role in social work education. *Journal of Teaching in Social Work, 4*(1), 113–128.

Perlman, H.H. (1962). The role concept and social casework: Some explorations II. *Social Service Review, 36*(1), 17–31.

Peterman, P., & Blake, R. (1986). The inappropriate BSW student. *Arete, 11*(1), 27–34.

Pincus, A., & Minahan, A. (1973). *Social work practice: Model and method.* Itasca: Peacock.

Ricks, F. (1991). Native sexual abuse counsellor: An empowerment training and healing model. *The Northern Review, 7, 112–129.*

Ryan, A.G. (1987). Tensions in trans-cultural Native education programs: Hurdles for the sensitive evaluator. *The Canadian Journal of Program Evaluation, 2*(1), 6979.

Schwartz, W. (1971). On the use of groups in social work practice. In W. Schwartz & S. Zalba (Eds.) *The practice of group work.* New York: Columbia University Press.

Shulman, L. (1987). The hidden group in the classroom: The use of group process in teaching group work practice. *Journal of Teaching in Social Work, 1*(2), 3–31.

Shulman, L. (1992). *The skills of helping: Individuals, families, and groups (3rd edition).* Itasca: Peacock.

Zapf, M.K. (1992). Educating social work practitioners for the North: A challenge for conventional models and structures. *The Northern Review, 7, 35–52.*

Zastrow, C. (1989). *The practice of social work (3rd Edition).* Chicago: Dorsey Press.

Chapter 4

Liberation or Assimilation

What are adult educators trying to do?

David Hannis

A Faltering Start

All journeys begin with the first step; we must make the road by walking (Bell, 1990; Trueblood, 1982). My venture into the unchartered waters of aboriginal education began in 1981, six years after coming to Canada from England. I had been invited by a provincial government department to deliver a workshop on time management to Metis settlement administrators from across rural northern Alberta. Despite meticulous planning, I found I was ill-prepared to meet the needs of my students. Before arriving in the small northern Alberta town where the workshop was to be delivered, I had scoured the relevant literature and had assembled what I thought was a reasonable summary of expert opinion on the topic. The fact that most of this material reflected the wisdom of people whose cultural backgrounds were significantly different from those of the people I would be teaching did not seem particularly relevant to me at the time. Truth is truth, after all. All the books I had read had been written by urban-based experts, usually male, probably none of whom had worked in or visited rural Alberta.

The day before my workshop, the area was hit by a blizzard. Undaunted, I headed out in a compact car, totally unsuited to the driving conditions I was to experience. Despite a few scares along the way, I checked into the town's only sizeable hotel later that night with only slightly elevated blood pressure. My hopes for a restful evening were quickly dashed when the band started up in the tavern. After dinner, I retired to my room, with its characteristic small town hotel smell, a unique blend of stale cigarette smoke, alcohol, and sickly air freshener. I awoke the next day tired and wishing I was back in Edmonton.

When I entered the classroom at the local vocational college after breakfast, the first thing I noticed was the broken clock on the wall. It seemed like an omen. There were no participants in the room, which was not a good sign either. I began to lose confidence. Up to that time, I had assumed that the administrators themselves had requested this workshop, but now I was not so sure. Maybe the choice of topic was more a reflection of the frustrations of distant white bureaucrats rather than a perceived need of the Native administrators themselves.

I needn't have worried; the workshop went fine. People kept coming and going all day, and I was mercilessly teased. A couple of participants dutifully took notes, but most did not. I learned a lot during that day, and so did some of the participants, I think. However, I did observe one thing, which I have since noticed many times while working with aboriginal students. I laugh at many of the same things they do. My sense of humour, born out of the oppressive British class system, is self-deprecating. It seems that humour helps us to come to terms with the injustices that surround us and the powerlessness we feel. It can also serve to remind us of our social status and deter us from getting ideas "above our stations." It can also help alleviate the stress of being educated away from our cultural roots. Whatever its purpose, for me, humour has proven to be an invaluable teaching tool that works with all students.

Consciousness Raising

In social work practice, a major threshold is often crossed when clients move from blaming themselves to identifying the external causes of their pain. Thus, the abused wife begins to become empowered only when she stops accepting responsibility for her partner's aggression and acknowledges that the roots of his dysfunctional behavior lie elsewhere. As long as the oppressed continue to believe the messages of their oppressors (typically, that they are evil, second class, inferior, stupid, lazy, or manipulative), they will continue to feel powerless, immobilized, apathetic, and worthless. When people and communities feel powerless, abuse flourishes.

A few years ago, shortly after Idi Amin had fled the country, I was asked to conduct a workshop on teacher effectiveness in Uganda. My students were well educated and many had attended Makarere University in Kampala. Until it had been plundered by Amin's troops, Makarere University was considered one of the best post-secondary institutions in Africa. Many of the workshop participants had travelled considerable distances, under difficult conditions and sometimes through terrorist controlled regions, to attend this session in Kampala. They represented a cross-section of different ethnic groups, some of whom had long histories of hostility toward each other. As a result, the atmosphere in the classroom was understandably tense. However, all participants appeared to be united in their desire to improve their teaching skills.

During my first class with the Ugandans, I talked a little about Canada and Canada's aboriginal people. I mentioned the treaties, the residential schools, the restricted curricula, the historical paternalism of the federal government, and various other social issues. At first they were stunned. How could there be poor people in a country as wealthy as Canada they asked? Then one of the quieter members observed that my description of the history of Canada's Native people paralleled their own colonial history. In the late nineteenth century, the British had come to Africa, along with other European powers, primarily for economic reasons. People from diverse ethnic backgrounds were collected together within arbitrarily defined countries, and boundaries were drawn with scant regard to existing tribal groupings. The schools, usually run by churches, offered a Western curriculum which was designed to train local people in the specific skills needed to ensure that the British entrepreneurs would receive a maximum economic return on their investments. Upward mobility for Ugandans was severely limited, and most educational institutions were less interested in nurturing their students' intellectual potential than in producing dutiful, efficient, technicians and civil servants. Canada's residential schools for Natives performed similar functions. Basically, Canada's residential schools were socialization and assimilation vehicles, whose primary purpose was to produce passive, uncritical citizens, aspiring to be white. Like their Ugandan counterparts, Canada's Natives have been the victims of colonialism, and they have paid a heavy price for other peoples' disregard of their plight. I travelled half way across the world to gain this insight.

Offering post-secondary educational opportunities to aboriginal students is a desirable goal, provided that teachers and students recognize that such learning has the potential to both liberate and oppress. Education is a two-edged sword. Historically, colonial powers have used education as a vehicle to stifle criticism and ensure conformity, and their curricula and educational standards have usually reflected male, urban, white, middle-class, European, capitalist values. In many parts of Africa exams are still produced and marked by people who live in other countries, thousands of miles away. Is, for example, a rural Ugandan woman's prowess at making English muffins, judged by scholars in Cambridge, relevant to her personal goals or those of her fragmented country?

By not controlling their educational and economic systems, many nominally independent former colonies remain answerable to their old colonial masters (Altbach, 1978; Carnoy, 1974, 1990). The potential for "white" society to continue its domination of aboriginal groups by retaining control of the educational system also exists in Canada. Educational institutions and aboriginal leaders have been hesitant to revise curricula for fear that it may lower academic standards and "water down" traditional programs. Roberts (1982) has described this educational dominance as "academic imperialism."

Historically, economically and socially disadvantaged groups have been skeptical of others' attempts to extend formal education to them, and Canadian aboriginal people have been no exception. In Britain, the earliest attempts at mass literacy were often more motivated by the desire to impose appropriate values and behaviours on the working classes than to create a more just society. However, as early reformers soon discovered, once people have learned to read, it becomes difficult to restrict their reading to authorized materials only. What started as a desire to teach people to read the Bible for instance, led to a flourishing demand for "seditious" publications and the rise of working-class political movements which eventually produced a shift in the balance of political power in Britain (Harrison, 1963; Jepson, 1973; Kelly, 1962).

A growing body of literature points to the potential of formal education, and by association formal educators, to perpetuate oppression. Some authors have made the distinction between "education" and "schooling;" the former refers to developing critical thinking abilities, while the latter involves memorizing and regurgitating other people's truths, without questioning its appropriateness or validity (Apple, 1979; Bourdieu, 1977; Bowles, 1976; Freire, 1972, 1981, 1985; Gramsci, 1973; Illich, 1971).

Aboriginal people have always been aware of the potential for "white" educational institutions to both liberate and oppress. Historically, schools for Native people frequently denigrated Native culture, punished and abused children, and did little more than prepare their charges for menial farm work and domestic service. Growing evidence suggests that, in the process, they caused considerable psychological and social damage. Mentors were rare. As a result, many Native students did poorly in school and were often burdened with a sense of guilt that has been perpetuated for generations. Those Native students who did well in school were quickly lost to white society, leaving weakened, stigmatised communities behind them (Barman, 1986; Ponting, 1980; Ward, 1986; Weaver, 1981).

Towards Cultural Reference

As a social worker and an adult educator, I am convinced that the key to a healthy future for aboriginal people lies through education, but not a narrowly defined education that merely provides learners with marketable technical skills. Such knowledge is culturally determined and can quickly become obsolete. If the education to which Native people are exposed is to be genuinely empowering, it must be culturally relevant, and it must provide learners with analytical thinking skills and creative problem-solving abilities. Incidentally, I also believe that this type of education is appropriate for non-aboriginal students as well. Education liberates; schooling oppresses.

Whenever I walk into a class of aboriginal students, particularly when the classroom is in a rural setting, I am immediately reminded of our differences. I am a white, urban-based, European-trained, male educator. My truth reflects my reality, but my reality is not the same as that of Alberta born, rural men and women from aboriginal backgrounds. It would be arrogant of me to claim that my knowledge is superior to that of my students. Most of the Native students I work with are women. Most of the textbooks we use are written by men who come from a different culture and often from a different country. We are only now becoming aware of the influence that gender and culture have on pedagogy and curriculum (Belenky, 1986; Carney, 1982; Dickinson, 1975; Doenan, 1987; D'Oyley, 1977; Freire, 1985; Gibson, 1986; Read, 1983; Restivo, 1990; Roberts, 1982; Saunders, 1976; Smith, 1990; Taylor, 1987; Tizard, 1988; Whyte, 1985).

When working with adult learners, regardless of their cultural background, I strive to be flexible, respectful, approachable, and human. I present my knowledge tentatively rather than as absolute truth, and I invite criticism and discussion. This style of teaching works for me personally and professionally. In developing this style, I have drawn primarily on the ideas of Freire (1972, 1981, 1985) and Knowles (1990). Of particular relevance to me is Freire's notion of learning as a process of "authentic dialogue," where the artificial boundaries between teacher and student are minimized, so that together we can strive collaboratively to reach a higher level of understanding. An effective teacher is a mentor who acts rather as a midwife, drawing forth the knowledge that lies buried within, in a safe and supportive way.

No matter how egalitarian a teacher's approach, students sometimes bring to the classroom behaviours that can get in the way of the learning process. People who have had negative experiences at school develop coping mechanisms that can interfere with intellectual risk taking. Students who fear humiliation and peer ridicule quickly learn not to expose their ignorance in the classroom. They must be reassured that such behaviours will not be tolerated or they will not rise to new intellectual challenges. Instead, they will revert to their old, dysfunctional survival strategies.

Effective teachers often interact socially with their students during class breaks. That is when some of the best learning can take place, and such interaction certainly helps to break down the barriers to learning. Good teachers do not flaunt their knowledge, but neither do they deny it. Adult educators do not always have to be nice; but they must always be fair, honest, sensitive, and congruent. Effective teachers strive to create a collaborative rather than a coercive learning environment. Their willingness to self-disclose and make themselves vulnerable greatly enhances this process and facilitates the development of trust.

The physical environment is also important to learning. Furniture should be arranged in ways that facilitate dialogue among students. Teachers must be sensitive to the communication patterns of different cultures and present assignments that provide opportunities for students to do some reflective writing and to link new ideas and concepts to their own realities. In such ways students and instructors become "critical co-investigators," collaboratively engaging in the pursuit of truth (Freire 1973, 1985).

Liberating instructors encourage students to speak out and to assert some control over the classroom agenda. Their goal always is to validate the student and the wisdom he or she brings to the classroom, to equip the student with critical thinking skills, and to provide the student with a lifelong love of learning. These are the tools of genuine empowerment.

My experience with teaching adults, and Native adults in particular, has taught me that achieving the goal of empowering these learners is not always easy. The impediments to learning that occur within any given class can include fatigue, low self-esteem, cognitive limitation, health difficulties, financial problems, relationship distractions, the fear of failure, the fear of success, and pregnancy (Restivo).

Most of the female Native students I work with have been effectively socialized to be "nice" and to avoid disagreement. Yet, according to Freire (Bell, 1990), "conflicts are the midwife of consciousness." Thus, when we ask women to challenge our truths or those of other experts, we are asking them to abandon years of socialization. It becomes an even greater challenge for students from cultures who have been taught not to challenge the wisdom of experts. This dilemma sometimes produces stressful inner tensions that can distort the learning process. When people who have been taught to remain silent suddenly speak out for the first time, their voices may be angry, accusing, contradictory, and ambivalent. Teachers must be careful not to become too defensive or leave students unsupported at critical times, otherwise they will retreat into an even deeper silence than before.

I remember one class where a relatively quiet student uncharacteristically spoke out with such force and anger that her peers responded with stunned silence. Although I was able to make some supportive statements, I too was surprised by the depth of feeling behind her remarks. I decided to seek her out after class. I caught up with her in the cafeteria where she was, as usual, sitting alone. She looked extremely distressed. I asked her what was going on for her, and she replied that she felt hurt, frightened, and vulnerable. As a victim of child sexual abuse, she had come from a dysfunctional family where she had learned that it was inappropriate to talk about feelings, and where everyone had secrets. Her peers' silence reminded her of those times. She felt alone and judged. I persuaded her to go back to class the following week, to tell her fellow students what she was feeling, and to ask them to explain their silence to her. She did just that, and her peers responded supportively and honestly. They told her that they had not been judging her but had been stunned, confused, embarrassed, and uncomfortable. A wonderful class discussion ensued, which subsequently led to a chain of positive consequences that I could never have predicted. I sensed that many students could identify with that student's pain, and being able to talk about it was a genuinely liberating experience for all of us. Thereafter, that student was a frequent contributor to classroom discussions, and she eventually became a competent, self-confident practitioner, able to pass her strength on to her clients and colleagues.

The End of the Beginning

Social workers have sometimes been accused of being "agents of social control" (Galper 1975, 1980). Under the guise of humanitarian concern, so the argument goes, they are ensuring the perpetuation of an unjust society, with its massive inequities in the distribution of wealth and privilege. Similar charges can be levelled at educators. However, our responsibility extends beyond merely equipping people with the technical skills they need to participate in the work force. We must ensure that they remain in touch with their own "humanness" and demonstrate compassion toward others. Sensitive, critical thinkers must also be encouraged to participate in society's democratic processes, not excluded from them.

I have been working with aboriginal students for more than ten years now, and my style of teaching is still evolving. I am still striving to become an expert on not being an expert, but that may take a few more years yet. In the meantime, I am clear what my role as an adult educator is, and I hope the students I work with are also. My purpose is to educate, not to school.

I, along with my colleagues at Grant MacEwan Community College, continue "to make the road by walking." I am not sure what's around the bend, but that's what makes life so exciting! And scary too!

References

Altbach, P. G., & Kelly, G. P (1978). *Education and colonialism. New York: Longman.*

Apple, M. (1979). *Ideology and curriculum.* London: Routledge and Kegan Paul.

Barman, J., Hebert, Y., & McCaskill, D. (1986). *Indian education in Canada.* Vols. *I & II.* Vancouver, BC: University of British Columbia.

Belenky, M. F., Clinchy, B. M., Goldberger, N. R., & Tarule, J. M.(1986). *Women's ways of knowing. The development of self, voice and mind.* New York: Basic Books.

Bell, B., Gaventa, J., & Peters, J. (Eds.). (1990). *We make the road by walking. Conversations on education and social change. Myles Horton and Paulo Freire.* Philadelphia, NJ: Temple University Press.

Bourdieu, P. (1977). *Reproduction in education, society and culture.* London: Sage.

Bowles, S., & Gintis, H. (1976). *Schooling in capitalistic America: Educational reform and the contradictions of economic life.* New York: Basic Books.

Carney, R. (1982). The road to Heart Lake: Native people, adult learners, and the future. *Canadian Journal of Native Education. 3*(3), Spring.

Carnoy, M. (1974). *Education as cultural imperialism.* New York: McKay.

Carnoy, M. (1990). *Education and social transition in the third world.* New Jersey: Princeton University Press.

Dickinson, L. (1975). *The immigrant school learner. A study of Pakistan pupils in Glasgow.* United Kingdom, Windsor.

Doenan, S. (1987). *Are teachers fair to girls?* New South Wales, Australia: Advance Publics.

D'Oyley, V., & Silverman, H. (Eds.). (1977). *Black students in urban Canada*. Toronto, ON: Citizenship Branch, Ministry of Culture and Recreation.

Freire, P. (1972). *Pedagogy of the oppressed*. New York: Herder and Herder.

Freire, P. (1981). *Education for critical consciousness*. New York: Continuum.

Freire, P. (1985). *The politics of education. Culture, power and liberation*. South Hadley, MA: Bergin & Garvey.

Galper, J.H. (1975). *The politics of social services*. Englewood Cliffs, NJ: Prentice Hall.

Galper, J.H. (1975). *Social work practice. A radical perspective*. Englewood Cliffs, NJ: Prentice Hall.

Gibson, A. (1986). *The unequal struggle. The findings of a West Indian research investigation into the under achievement of West Indian children in British schools*. London: Centre for Carribean Studies.

Gramsci, A. (1973). *Letters from prison*. New York: Harper & Row.

Harrison, J. F. C. (1963). *Learning and living. A study in the history of the English adult education movement*. London: Routledge and Kegan Paul.

Illich, I. (1971). *Deschooling society*. New York: Harper and Row.

Jepson, N. A. (1973). *The beginnings of university adult education. Policy and problems*. London: Michael Joseph.

Kelley, M. L., & Nelson, C. H. (1986). A non-traditional education model with Indian indigenous social service workers. *Canadian Journal of Native Education. 13*(3), Spring.

Kelly, T. (1962). *A history of adult education in Great Britain*. Liverpool: Liverpool University Press.

Knowles, M. (1990). *The adult learner: A neglected species*. Houston, TX: Gulf.

Machado, A. (1982). *Selected poems.* (A.S. Trueblood, Trans.). Cambridge, MA: Harvard University Press.

Ponting, J. R. & Gibbins, R. (1980). *Out of irrelevance.* Toronto, ON: Butterworth.

Read, E. J. (1983). Education programs for disadvantaged adults. A case study-project morning star. *Canadian Journal of Native Education. 10*(2), Winter.

Restivo, G. (1990). *Yellowhead Tribal Council, Grant MacEwan Community College, Social Work Program, Spruce Grove. Four-year report (1986-90).* Edmonton, AB: Grant MacEwan Community College.

Roberts, H. (1982) *Culture and adult education. A study of Alberta and Quebec.* Edmonton, AB: University of Alberta Press.

Saunders, D. (1976). Project morning star: An interim assessment. *Canadian Journal of Indian Education, 3*(2), Winter.

Smith, D. (1990). *The conceptual practices of power: A feminist sociology of knowledge.* Toronto, ON: University of Toronto Press.

Taylor, M. J. (1987). *Chinese pupils in Britain. A review of research into the education of pupils of Chinese origin.* Windsor, United Kingdom: NFER-Nelson Publ.

Tizard, B. (1988). *Young children at school in the inner city.* Hove, United Kingdom: Lawrence Erlbaum Association.

Ward, M. S. (1986). Indian education, policy and politics, 1972-1982. *Canadian Journal of Native Education, 13*(2), Winter.

Weaver, S. (1981). *Making Canadian Indian policy. The hidden agenda 1968-70.* Toronto, ON: University of Toronto.

Whyte, J. (1985). *Girl friendly schooling.* London: Methuen.

Chapter 5

Being There

Applying Rogerian concepts in the classroom

Marianne Wright

Several years ago, I had the pleasure of attending a workshop hosted by Dr. Carl Rogers. Here before me was one of the grandfathers of the helping profession. His interactions with his audience truly reflected his beliefs. He was, to use his own term, congruent. During question period, someone asked Dr. Rogers what he considered was the most important skill a therapist could have. His answer: "Being there." This response seemed rather disappointing and simplistic to me at the time. However, as a therapist and a teacher, I have since pondered what he meant by that brief statement. The more I have studied, pondered, and practised "being there," the more I have come to realize how truly difficult this skill is. When teaching in an outreach setting, it seems to be almost impossible. However, I have also come to believe that, in working with indigenous populations, it is essential to "be there."

What does "being there" really mean, and how can we translate this concept into our teaching style? Rogers believes that "being there" encompasses the three conditions necessary to successful therapy. He also believes these same conditions are essential to successful teaching. The three conditions are congruence, unconditional positive regard, and empathy.

In this case, congruence means being genuine and real. It seems simple enough. Yet on closer scrutiny, it actually means, "when my experiencing of this moment is present in my awareness and when what is present in my awareness is present in my communication" (Rogers, 1980, p. 15). In other words, as an instructor, I must be self-aware, tuned into my own feelings and thoughts at this moment, and then this awareness must be communicated to others through both verbal and nonverbal communication.

My first experience with congruency in teaching began on a reserve in Southern Alberta over 10 years ago. The subject was family dynamics; the time of year was winter. I was congruent enough to share my apprehension of my new situation; however, I was assured that the co-trainer who would be travelling with me was an experienced instructor. Unfortunately, when this co-trainer became ill, a new and completely inexperienced co-trainer was hired to accompany me.

We left Edmonton on a cold, blustery day and not 100 kilometers from home, we had a flat tire. Was this a preview of my teaching career? Two hours later, and much colder, we headed south again. We arrived late at a building that looked like it had been lifted out of the 1950s and simply plunked down onto the plains. I was not far wrong—the building was an old residential school where various religious groups, under government approval, brought Native children to learn the white man's knowledge and religion. What an irony! Here I was, another white person, again sent to teach the "Natives." As we pulled into the driveway, I noticed blood was dripping out of the trunk of one of the cars in the parking lot. I was certain I was entering a different world—and this one appeared hostile. I walked into the classroom where the students were waiting. They were all Native. I was the only white person. But I was the instructor, and I had the power of grades.

Thus began my teaching career and my struggle with congruence, unconditional positive regard, and empathy. I taught them family dynamics à la Virginia Satir. They taught me to be real (congruent). On the third day of the course, my students not so tactfully informed me that I was a failure as Virginia Satir. The course was way over their heads, and they did not give a damn about the grades. There went my power. I would like to tell you that at that moment a magical transformation occurred, and I became congruent on the spot. However, I had long since given up on miracles. What I did instead was struggle. I asked myself, was I a failure as a teacher after only three days? I needed to change, but change what? Like most new teachers, all of my wisdom had come from books. Now I had to learn to find the wisdom within me. I had to become aware of my own emotions and thoughts, which included my prejudices and fears.

Gaining the awareness of these feelings was uncomfortable and difficult, but even more difficult was the task of sharing, where appropriate, these thoughts and feelings with my students. This made me even more vulnerable. As teachers, we often carry around an idea of what it means to be a teacher—wisdom, knowledge, and respect. If I am congruent or real, maybe the students won't like me or respect me, or maybe they will discover that I don't really know all that much. And instructors want to be liked. Slowly, over the years, I have learned to "be there" and be real with the students. This ability puts us both on a more equal footing and allows us to learn from one another.

When discussing learning, Rogers states that:

> "perhaps the most basic of these essential attitudes is realness, or genuineness. When the facilitator is a real person, being what he or she is, entering into relationships with the learners without presenting a front or a facade, the facilitator is much more likely to be effective. This means that the feelings that the facilitator is

experiencing are available to his or her awareness, that he or she is able to live these feelings, to be them, and able to communicate them if appropriate. It means that the facilitator comes into a direct, personal encounter with the learners, meeting each of them on a person-to-person basis. It means that the facilitator is *being,* not denying himself or herself. The facilitator is *present* to the students."
Rogers, 1980, (p. 271)

I will be forever grateful to those students who taught me about congruence during that cold week in January. When I became congruent and shared my fear of the blood dripping out of the trunk of that car, they merely laughed. A woman had shot an elk on her way to class and put it in the trunk of her car where she knew it would freeze quickly. In that way, she was able to maintain her food supply and enhance her education at the same time.

Unconditional positive regard is a basic tenet in the social work profession. This term generally implies the acceptance or non-possessive prizing of another human being. Rogers (1980) states, "I think of this attitude as a prizing of each learner, a prizing of his or her feelings, opinions, and person. It is a caring for the learner, but a nonpossessive caring. It is an acceptance of this other individual as a separate person, a respect for the other as having worth in his or her own right" (p. 271).

Too often, as instructors, we look out on a "sea of faces" and forget that this sea is full of unique individuals, each striving along their own journey through life. We must learn to see the individual, not the "Native" student. Yes, we need to understand their culture, but we must also understand how these unique individuals experience their culture.

I had the privilege of again teaching this same group of students from southern Alberta a few months later. Several students told me that they were impressed with how much I had learned. I thanked them for teaching me. They invited me to a "sweat," and then shared with me some of their personal and cultural beliefs about that custom. When they invited me to attend, they did not know that I was afraid of enclosed spaces and did not like saunas. Here was another of life's ironies. We were talking about fear, and I was waxing eloquently on overcoming fear; then came their invitation. I respected their invitation and I respected them. How could I not go to the sweat? Indeed it was an honour to be asked. If I prized them and myself, I had to honour their request. I did, and again I thanked them for their teaching. I think that is part of prizing others—a recognition that if we are real and congruent, our students will become our teachers. We can learn from one another.

Prizing and respecting, however, does not mean accepting negative or destructive behavior. We accept the person, but not necessarily the behavior. For instructors, this may mean halting a disruptive class, and seeking out an understanding of the negative behavior. Too often, instructors judge students on their behavior, which emphasizes the power difference and causes resentments that can lead to difficulties in learning. By accepting the person, we show respect. By not accepting disruptive or destructive behavior, we also show respect.

Empathy is the last skill required for "being there." Rogers (1980) defines this skill as being with another person for a time where "you lay aside your own views and values in order to enter another world without prejudice. In some sense it means that you lay aside your self; this can only be done by persons who are secure enough in themselves that they know they will not get lost in what may turn out to be the strange or bizarre world of the other, and that they can comfortably return to their own world when they wish" (p. 143). When we apply this definition to teaching, we begin to see how very difficult it might be to practice empathy in the classroom.

As instructors, how can we stand in our students' shoes and grade and evaluate them at the same time? The key to this situation is that we must, in a sense, wear two hats. As a teacher, I need to understand how the students feel and learn, yet I must also remain aware of my role as their instructor. This balance is especially difficult to maintain in outreach situations. I remember hearing the terribly sad stories of these students' lives—lives filled with poverty, abuse from parents, residential schools, and escapes into violence and alcoholism. At times, I could feel their pain. It was so easy to get caught up in this pain (as we often do with clients) and spend the class time sharing those experiences. I often got lost in their world and forgot about my own.

So how do we find a balance where we can hear their pain, and yet direct these experiences toward learning and growth? Recently, I was teaching a course on Mental Health Intervention to a group of outreach students. It was the first morning of class, and I was presenting the course outline. I was trying very hard to squeeze in as much material as possible, because it is a short course that contains a lot of information. I had been told that there had been some class problems, but that the students would not be disruptive. As I proceeded, I heard a student crying. I knew it was not a result of the material I was presenting and was probably related to some unfinished business within the class. As instructors, we are often faced with such moments of decision. Do I ignore the situation and carry on in order to meet my own instructional needs, or do I confront the issue and, if so, am I willing to become involved in the process? Trusting the students, I followed their lead when they requested time to process the incident. The student was upset because someone close to her had died, and she had not received any condolences from her fellow classmates. She was hurt. I asked the students about their behavior. Why hadn't they responded? As each student shared, it became obvious that they had all been painfully touched by this student's loss. Loss after loss was shared, and then we reflected on what might happen if she was a client? How do we deal with loss? What happens if we deny loss? And thus we returned to my subject—our mental health. They became their own teachers, and I was merely the instrument of their learning.

Sometimes, it is easier to judge, and after all, evaluation is a part of an instructor's job. Initially, I found myself asking, "What is wrong with these students? Why don't they show basic kindness?" But once I was willing to suspend my judgement and really listen, I understood. Rogers (1980) states, "this attitude of standing in the students' shoes, of viewing the world through their eyes, is almost unheard of in the classroom. But when the teacher responds in a way that makes the students feel *understood*—not judged or evaluated—this has a tremendous impact" (p. 272).

Another trap that non-Native instructors sometimes fall into is the "wanna be" syndrome. As I was teaching Natives and reading Native literature, I became impressed with and inspired by Native spirituality—so much so, that I wanted to be Native. If I could be more like them, then I might also feel more accepted and less insecure. But, as Rogers reminds us, if we enter the world of the other, we must be careful not to lose touch with our own world. I must be secure enough in my own world so that I can hear their stories, feel their pain, respect their heritage, and yet never forget who I am and why I am. As their instructor, I am there to facilitate their learning process, and hopefully in that process, we will both learn and all of us will be touched and enriched by our time together.

My own discovery of how these Rogerian concepts apply to teaching Native students is echoed by Guntars J. Grintals (1980) who states, "Hence, no approach other than what is generally described as a 'Client-Centered Counselling' would appear to provide the process, and the characteristics congruent with the self-concept, cultural makeup, and the nature of man as perceived by the North American Indians" (p. 29).

Perhaps what I have learned from Carl Rogers was already known and practised by ancient Native spiritualists. Brod Steiger (1984), in his book *Indian Medicine Power* offers this perspective:

> "Indian medicine should have gotten proper credit for theories including the psychoanalytic ideas of Sigmund Freud, analytic thinking of Carl Jung, holistic or individual approaches of Alfred Adler, the psychology of consciousness of William James, the client-centered perspectives of Carl Rogers, and the Gestalt approach suggested by Frederick Perls."

"There was nothing more respected and cherished than the spirit of a person. This was sacred because a person's spirit was like the Great Spirit. That dignity of a person must always be held sacred as Indian people have always believed. It is held sacred by respect and love for each self and all around the self" (p. 193).

References

Grintals, G.J. (1980). *Indian culture and traditional social work effectiveness.* Unpublished manuscript.

Rogers, C. (1980). *A way of being.* Boston, MA: Houghton Miffin Co.

Steiger, B. (1984). *Indian medicine power.* Boston, MA: Para Research.

Chapter 6

Who Are You?

How the Aboriginal classroom sparks fundamental issues in human development

Pam Colorado

The Rapture Of The North

Have you ever stood beneath a star-studded boreal sky? The feeling is ecstasy. A full moon iridesces blue on crystalline snow, and your breath mingles with the cries of distant wolves. Stout spruce point like inky fingers to the heavens, and minus 40 becomes a spiritual experience. It takes just seconds to savor this epiphenomena. If you stop to think about what is happening and leave your total awareness for even a moment, you will fall into a sleep and die. Being aware of the danger is no protection; the beauty and feeling is so good it is impossible to ignore. This is the Rapture, and I knew it would be there waiting for me.

What Brings Us To This Work?

The Time Air flight was bumpy. I anxiously looked out of the tiny window onto windswept patches of frozen brown prairie soil. It had been nearly five years since I last worked in the far North. Memories of the Yukon and Arctic Slope came to mind. Wearily, I recalled my futile efforts to stave off the annihilation of Native knowledge and culture. I remembered the intense passion I felt while defending the beautiful land, water, trees, and animals. I thought about the Native people, whose capacity for suffering seemed endless. Images of their persecutors came to mind—the grey-faced, suited bureaucrats, the ubiquitous loggers, the slick oil men, the compromised paper chiefs, and the deaf-eared social workers, who turned away from the agony of the people. I did not want to face this situation again. I hated and feared the approaching vortex. But somewhere, deep inside of me, there was an excitement about this new project. Maybe, during the intervening years, I had learned something that could be of use, could finally make a difference.

I considered my resources. I had a basic knowledge of Dene life and culture because of my previous work in the Yukon. I had grown up next to Algonquian speaking people and had attended many Cree gatherings. Still, I had been to High Level only once before, and I wondered what experiences lie ahead for my colleague and me. Kim Zapf and I had known each other for several years. Although we both taught at the University of Calgary, we had never worked together before. Now circumstances were thrusting the two of us into an intense teaching experience. We were to prepare and present two social work courses for Grant MacEwan Community College's Social Work Outreach program to Native students in High Level, Alberta.

The course hours had been doubled to accommodate the cross-cultural context; our week-long teaching blocks meant that we would be in the classroom together for a full 40 hours! The notion of 24 people packed into a windowless classroom for such an extensive period of time seemed overwhelming. There was a sense of being consumed by this teaching project; a feeling heightened by the fact that instructors had to be flown in and billeted in local hotels. Outside instructors in a small northern community have little to do after class except think about and prepare for their next day's work.

When an educational experience is this intimate, certain boundaries must be established. This was a complicated challenge because the course was intended for Native students. That meant that two sets of social rules would apply in any given situation. The Western protocols were quite clear; the setting was going to be a classroom, and class rules would be based on a standard teacher–student relationship. The Native protocols were not nearly as simple. A noted Lakota scholar, Vine Deloria, has suggested that, for Natives, the purpose of education "is to understand and complete our relationship" with all living things (Deloria 1986). Thus, our small classroom in High Level represented the convergence of Western linear thought and its hierarchical pedagogical form with the holistic, processural knowledge system of the global indigenous family. Kim and I were to stand between these two historically antagonistic ways of thinking!

Meeting & Greeting

At first blush, one might wonder why anyone would agree to enter into such an educational conundrum. The answer is simple. Social work is the only discipline that views the individual within his or her environment. The High Level class challenged us to integrate the social work perspective within a Native context. It gave us the opportunity to try to merge the Western mind with the nature-based mind of Native Americans. We knew that these divergent thinking patterns have kept Native and Western people separated, from their first moment of contact until today. Thus, this meeting of minds in our small northern classroom represented a microcosm of the larger global struggle to deal with the devastation "triggered by the worldwide dominance of the Euro-American capitalist-industrial economies, continuing today to ravage the biosphere with ever-increasing efficiency and intensity." Both Kim and I sensed the depth and quality of this event. Although we never mentioned it (until after the course was completed), both of us had grave doubts as to whether or not our social work training and my own Native teachings would be enough to see us through this experience.

How We Greet Each Other

Because Native Americans have been invaded by, and continue to be threatened by, the Western world, addressing the issues of touch, communication styles, boundaries, and identity was the first order of business. The importance of this rule became evident to me when I undertook a project to research the roles and functions of Reserve alcoholism counsellors. Richard, a Tlingit who had adopted me into his family, took me to meet (and presumably, to interview) the Reverend Cyrus Peck. At age 72, Cyrus was the esteemed head of the Eagle Clan. He was fluent in his language and a published author on his culture. When you gazed on his stern countenance and snow-white hair, you could not help but think of an eagle. My meeting with him was an awesome experience, and it drove home the Native imperative of relationship. The encounter was so vivid, it seems as if it happened only yesterday.

Four hours of seaplane and ferry travel through rough coastal weather had chilled me to the bone. My slicker and gum boots had trapped cold sweat on my body, and I longed for the warmth of the cedar fire that was sure to be blazing in Cyrus Peck's home. Peck was the village patriarch. He was 72, a traditional Chief, an ordained minister, and head of the Eagle Clan. He looked like an eagle, sitting there in his over-stuffed chair. His white hair stood in thick shocks on his head, and his shirt was draped like dark wings on his aging body. His sharp eyes were penetrating, and I felt acutely uncomfortable under his intense gaze.

A year earlier, I had married into a neighboring tribe. I was new to the Coastal culture and was relieved to have Richard, a Tlingit leader, serve as a mediary in my research work. Based on my tribe's custom, I had prepared an offering for the Elder. Richard introduced us. "Uncle, this is my sister, Pam Colorado-Morrison. Pam, this is Cyrus Peck, Eagle Clan." Then Richard gave my offering to Cyrus. The old man held the small bundle in his hands for a moment and then set it aside. Looking at me, Cyrus said quietly, "Morrison, huh? Hydaburg. We have a nephew over there...."

Several minutes went by, I could hear the ticking of the clock and the crackling of the wood in the stove. Cyrus was seated next to the fire, blocking the heat from Richard and me. I was nearly shaking with chill. I wished the Elder would ask us to sit down. Gradually, I became aware that Richard was looking at me. Somehow the ball had landed in my court. I racked my brain trying to think of what I should do. What was expected? What was the old man waiting for? Suddenly, I realized that he was waiting for me to identify the 'nephew.' Now, I was no longer cold. I was so scared I was sweating. I knew this was some kind of test, and I silently prayed that my brains wouldn't let me down. Suddenly a name popped in my mind. It was the name of my husband's Grandfather, a man who had died 20 years before I met my husband! "Paul Morrison," I offered. "Yes," the old man said, "sit down."

Shaking with relief, I sank onto the couch. A feeling of joy came over me. I had been tested and I had made the cut. Actually, Cyrus Peck was extremely kind to me. He spoke in English and insisted that we clarify the basis of our relationship before we consider any type of undertaking. I was grateful that my Grandfather-in-law had been a good man. His good life and my knowledge of him were the keys that opened the door of friendship and cooperation for Cyrus and me.

Because I had successfully demonstrated that I knew who I was and how I was related to the Tlingit and to the Elder, I was allowed to take the next step—making my request. I explained the nature of my research and asked Cyrus to help me to define the function and role of reserve-based counsellors. He not only shared his thoughts with me, he also gave me a typewritten curriculum! He used two methods for sharing this curriculum information. First, he gave me the actual document, which contained an itemized list of the courses as well as an indication of their content areas. (This curriculum will be found in Addendum A at the end of this chapter.) Second, he guided me through a process for teaching the curriculum. To accomplish this task, he insisted that we interact in accordance with traditional protocol.

The Washing Ceremony

Relationships are governed by the principle of respect. *"Sha awdan'e,* self-respect, that is something we have lost," Cyrus said. It is certainly true in the case of Native and Western relationships. This loss of self-respect is nearly palpable in the social work classroom, and it pertains to both instructor and student alike. Peck taught me that we must acknowledge what has happened between our peoples and face the personal consequences of being caught in this juggernaut. If we do this, we will become whole. The Elder shared a ceremony for healing the historical wound, which I will share with you. First, he compelled me to be clear about my identity, about the relationship that guided us (he was an Uncle to me). Then he introduced the source of the problem that brought us together in a powerful way. He produced a document that the Tlingit were forced to sign.

> WE, the undersigned, Alaska Natives of _____, Alaska, hereby declare that we have given up our old tribal relationships; that we have given up all claim to or interest in tribal and communal houses; that we live in one-family houses in accordance with the customs of civilization; that we observe the marriage laws of the United States; that our children take the name of the father and belong equally to the father and mother, and that the rights of the maternal uncle to direct the children are no longer recognized, and that in the case of the death of either parent, we recognize the laws of the United States relative to the inheritance of property; that we have discarded the Totem and recognize the Stars and Stripes as our only emblem; and that we are self-supporting and law-abiding people.
>
> We therefore believe we have fulfilled all requirements necessary to citizenship in the United States, and we respectfully request the Congress of the United States to pass a law granting to us the full rights of citizenship.
>
> State of Alaska Government Document

Although this action was unconstitutional, the Territorial Government imposed it on all Indians who desired to keep any of their lands. The Act required White people to countersign their statements. This Act destroyed Native culture, identity, and self-respect. It also freed thousands of acres of Native land from communal ownership and passed them into the public domain or into the hands of private businesses and the Church. The same process of expropriation occurred in Canada through the Potlatch Law, the Indian Act, and the residential schools system.

This document is concrete evidence of the problems that exist between Western and Native people. It establishes the fact that their relationship has been built on power and domination, which has since been maintained by a one-way communication flow. The typical social work educator perpetuates this domination by pretending to teach presence, while at the same time, models behaviors of extreme alienation. For example, instructors ignore the history of genocide, which permits them to teach from a monocultural paradigm while working in a bicultural setting, or they ignore the spiritual/metaphysical aspects of causality (the essence of the Native mind), because the Western belief is that spirituality can be separated from physicality.

From a Native point of view, the effects of Western domination include a profound diffusion of identity, self-hate or fear of one's culture, unconsciously vacillating between Western and Native behaviors, and the loss of a cultural vision, which is critical to the formation of one's life. In my own case, I was frightened by the prospect of teaching from a Native perspective. I feared ridicule, chastisement, and shame even though I knew that the traditional values were strong and good and would serve as a powerful integrating tool for all of us. Nevertheless, I had never shared these concepts with Northern Native students, nor had I ever taught social work from my own perspective, that is, from a Native mind. For years, I had been teaching social work courses as if I were a Western person! I wanted to be myself with this class; to teach from my own Native mind, to impart integral Native teachings, but at the same time, respect the curriculum of the

Western social work program. To do this, I needed Kim to monitor the Western teachings and to help me link or point out the divergences between the Native and the Western content.

True to Western form, Kim and I worked out a curriculum, assignments, and grading procedures. We reviewed them with the class on the first day. Then we introduced the concept of Native social work and explained that we would be teaching the course from both perspectives. The tension in the classroom was palpable. The Native students questioned the value, approach, and methods of Native social work. A few were quietly supportive; a few more were openly hostile to the idea; most tried to ignore the issue. The deep identity conflict made me want to weep; it also put a great deal of pressure on Kim. Should he trust me and support this bicultural approach to Native social work education? Or should he reduce the conflict in the classroom by insisting that we stick to a purely Western approach? He decided to stand by me.

Now the pressure was on me. I needed to think of an appropriate Native protocol for teaching in a bicultural arena. It wasn't easy. Native knowledge has been eroded; we face circumstances today that our ancestors never imagined. If there were protocols for bicultural teaching, I certainly wasn't aware of them. Nevertheless, I recognized that Kim and I had been presented a wonderful possibility—to rediscover and revive ancient knowledge about social work. In this context, I recalled Reverend Peck's traditional teaching method and process for counselling; it became my curriculum guide.

A Traditional Process For Counselling
As presented by Reverend Cyrus Peck, Tlingit Chief

Permission to Share
Native knowledge is sacred. It is the inheritance of the Native community. Certain people, such as Mr. Peck, may share their knowledge under special circumstances. The use of this information, either in whole or in part, is unlawful if the protocols for its transfer are not met. This legal criteria also applies to tribal traditions, and Western law upholds the intellectual property rights of Native people. The knowledge I

am sharing here is mine to share because I followed the proper tradition, and because Reverend Peck was satisfied that I was a suitable recipient of this information. (Through family ties, he is my Uncle.) Thus, he instructed me:

> "The curriculum I gave you is a key to the Native way of living. If you are going to counsel the Native people, know these. Know this by heart."

Social work educators may use this model as a conceptual aid. It can be used as a reading assignment for students, which may serve as a springboard for discussion, or it can be used as a vehicle for developing and enlisting the support of local, traditional Native people. It must not be fragmented or decontextualized in any way.

The Process

"When you start, start as I did."

- Who are you?
- What is your crest (clan)?
- *T'ak dein toon?* Are you living it?

"Give instruction, information. To teach *Shaa awdan'e,* self-respect, that's the key work in Tlingit. Self respect goes back a long ways." Provide information to explain the loss of identity such as the Agreement the Tlingit were forced to sign.

Use repetition. After giving information, ask again, "Who are you? You see, the identity is something that we have lost and that is something that the young generation is looking for, searching for."

Encourage the person to ask, Who am I? What am I doing here? What is my future? Because I know my crest, I know who I am. My Native name is _____. Know who you are, and if you're Native, know your Tlingit, Haida, or Tsimshian name."

"Continue the process. Ask again, 'Who are you? What is your crest? Dog Salmon crest, for example? Yes, Dog Salmon is your crest.' Now give information and education—Dog Salmon crest. Yes, Dog Salmon is your crest. That's something that you have lost sight of and you were not told by your mother or father because they were discouraged...It's our way, we are Natives and that's the way we have been created and this is something that has been lost..."

Now, continue the process. "Who are you? What is your crest? What is your (Indian) name? Why are you here?"

Relationship is the nexus. "Finally come to the point. Why are you like this when your great uncles are self-respecting people? The spirit of the uncles, the spirit of our grandparents are with us. They are everywhere, all you have to do is remind me of it. What this will do, is bring me back to our relationship. This is the key, to remind me and others of our self-respect. *Shaa awdan'e. Shaa awdan'e.* Self-respect with your head high because you know who you are."

Illness or misfortune derives from imbalance with the environment. Therefore, ground the presenting issue with the environment. "We are living in an age that's never the same as one before. We are living in an age, a unique time. Science, people travelling in space. People are living in fear of nuclear power. There are powers out there that are ready to destroy our human beings; alcohol is part of it."

"We are a nation. The Tlingit people are a nation. We can say with pride and hold our heads up high, we are a nation that has never known alcohol...it was not a part of our life, ever! When I see a young man staggering, my heart goes out to him. He doesn't know how to handle things. The White man says if you're going to drink, learn how to drink. Learn when to quit. Who learns when to quit? I haven't seen it!"

Now, you go further in a man's life, "Who is your Uncle?" (The Tlingit follow an avuncular system) "Where is he? What is he doing?" The Uncle is obligated to train him because he is of the same Clan. The Uncle, because it is his nephew, pulls him out of bed and getting dressed says, "So this for a day, this is your work day." And you do it! This is something we lost that we must bring back...the authority of the Uncle over the younger generation.

Now, "Who are we? Where do I come from? It is important to know. We are a nation, we have been a nation. We are still a nation! Sovereignty is the question."

The process concludes. Peck shares one or two traditional stories that highlight and summarize the healing process that is now concluding. These stories provide standards for future living. Finally, Peck asks the educators a question:

"We are dealing with spiritual problems, with things unseen and therefore, your results cannot be measured by a yardstick...So for that reason, your approach to individuals is very important. The Tlingit Nation has beliefs. Beliefs are known to strengthen the core of an individual. What is it you believe?"

"What you believe is important because your body reacts to your beliefs. Tlingit have Ways, Words of Power, that bring people back to themselves. *Shaa awdan'e she, Shaa awdan'etin.*"

"That's the theme striking in your minds today. Self respect. *Shaa awdan'etin.*"

Summary

Travelling to the far North in January will challenge even the most hearty individuals. For social work educators, the stress of travel and climate is merely preparation for the challenge of the Native classroom. Preparing to teach in the North requires that we clarify our purpose and be strong in our intent, and coping with the cross-cultural experience requires that we deeply examine our personal values, carefully assess the consequences of our presence on a fragile environment, and look closely at the shadow side of our work. To this end, Kim Zapf and I met every day to review these items. We also established the following guidelines for our work in High Level:

1. We recognized and declared the limits of Western social work practice and social work education with Native people. We set these limitations because the results of social work practice and teaching have previously been used to justify genocide.

2. There is no established infrastructure for teaching social work from the perspective of both Native and Western world views. If we had wanted to use Western social work methods to assimilate Native people into an uncritical acceptance of a foreign model of social work, we had a huge infrastructure from which to work. But

there is no infrastructure for linking and translating bicultural knowledge and converting such scientific knowledge into action.

3. We accepted the scientific pluralism and relinquished a monocultural view of social work by:
   - assuming that Native cultures contain a social work; and
   - seeking out the traditional knowledge of the participating Native peoples. This effort constituted an act of reconciliation; it grounded and enriched the Native half of our bicultural approach to teaching.

4. We abandoned the dependency theory of social work education, which claims that Native students in rural, traditional (often sustainable) communities must first become Western in order to be competent social work practitioners. We used the additional class hours to discover, articulate, and renew a traditional Native approach to social work.

5. The principles of social justice, egalitarianism, and a true partnership among the students, the instructors, and the Program Coordinator would be used to guide our process.

To further these goals, Dr. Zapf and I negotiated a team-teaching approach. Kim Zapf was responsible for presenting the Western social work content, and I assumed responsibility for providing the Native social work content. Our students became active partners in this two-way educational experience.

Addendum A

The Tlinglit Nation – Special Subject and Course Curriculum

Developed by Reverend Cyrus Peck

Reverend Peck states that these areas constitute the competence that all village-based counsellors, who work with the Tlingit people, should have.

I.
- The history and territory of the Tlingit prior to the coming of the white man
- Migrations of the Tlingit
- Vocabulary

II.
- Village Life
- Vocabulary

III.
- The Tlingit People
  a. The nation
  b. The Eagle and Raven
  c. Clan relationships
- Vocabulary

IV.
- Family Life
  a. Women
  b. Men
  c. Interrelations of the family
  d. Whose children?
- Vocabulary

V.
- Making a Living
  a. Trap Line
  b. Fishing
  c. Hunting
  d. Trade
- Vocabulary

VI.
- Living Art of the Tlingit
  - a. Statesmanship
  - b. Rhetoric
  - c. Ceremonials in statecraft
  - d. Formal artwork
- Vocabulary

VII.
- Living Art of the Tlingit
  - a. Mythology and legend
  - b. Medicine men and the occult
  - c. Crafts and skills
  - d. Fun and games
  - e. Ceremonial entertainment
- Vocabulary

VIII.
- Life Crises
  - a. Birth
  - b. Coming of age
  - c. Marriage
  - d. Taking a spouse
  - e. Assumption of ceremonial life-role
  - f. Special ceremonies
  - g. Death
  - h. After death
- Vocabulary

IX.
- The Tlingit at war and in peace
- Vocabulary

X.
- Relations with other nations
  - a. Other Indian Nations
  - b. European nations
    - Governmental
    - Religious impact
    - Educational efforts
- Vocabulary

XI
- Test

Chapter 7

Coherence

A process of social work education with Aboriginal students

Pam Colorado

Prologue

Every calender system must account for the extra days in its annual cycle. For Native people, these time / space moments occur when the sun is directly overhead and makes no shadow. These times are often referred to as dead days and represent a powerful, creative suspension in time. You need to move carefully, deliberately, and ceremonially—the magnification and amplification of the consequences of your actions may be awesome...

Introduction

By the time we left town, it was after seven in the evening. William Pelech, the Program Coordinator, his son John, and I were driving west of High Level, Alberta to the Chinchaga

River. Suddenly, William stepped on the brakes. There, in front of the van was a Native man, inebriated and staggering on the highway. We had nearly hit him. As we drove on, the brilliant shadowless rays of the Midnight sun penetrated our line of vision. I experienced a light-headed feeling that lasted the remainder of the 40-kilometre ride. In the rear view mirror, black storm clouds gathered.

As we stepped out of the van, a swarm of mosquitoes enveloped us. William and John ran for the swimming hole; I walked quickly up river. My purpose was clear: I wanted permission to be in this land, and I needed to strengthen my "Medicine" so that I could teach in the best manner possible.

I had no Elder to support me. I was on my own, as I had so often been before in my traditional Native life. I wished that my Grandfather had lived longer, that he had taught me more. The buzzing mosquitoes urged me on. Something in the smoothness of the grey, waterworn rock and the slow eddy of the water next to it invited me to rest. I smudged, cleansed myself, and made an offering. No response. I continued. While making my request, I took my Medicine Bag from around my neck and immersed it in the cold moving water. The feeling was very intense. Still, no response. I lifted the bag and held it toward the storm clouds in the West, the direction of the ancestors. I called out, "Do you hear me?" A straight bolt of lightening flashed from the clouds to the river in front of me. "Will you give me permission to be here, and will you help me to do this work?" Again, lightening tore across the sky toward the earth. Quickly, I gave thanks and bundled up my things. Then, as I wheeled around, I gave a wild whoop of joy and placed the necklace back around my neck.

Halfway home, the storm caught us. Violent winds and rain buffeted the van. Ragged bolts of lightening streaked across the sky. Between rounds of lightening, blackness devoured the road. In the light of the next bolt, William hit the brakes. There, less than a metre away stood an enormous Snow Owl. It turned, looked at us, and then unfolded its wings, which extended beyond the width of the van. In three powerful strokes it was gone! Shaken, we said little, but we stopped to leave an offering of acknowledgement and agreement.

The Snow Owl Process – A guide for restoring spirit and identity in the Aboriginal classroom

In the old days, education was an integral aspect of Native life. The community welcomed each new child and encouraged the child to find his or her place in the community. Even the traditional architecture of the home provided lessons in logic, mathematics, astronomy, and social relations. Today, when Native people want to help other Native people, they must work within, and be credentialed by, a foreign culture that nurtures the same disruption it proposes to heal. It is a painful reality, but to deny this reality only perpetuates and exacerbates the problem.

Native ceremonial life provides a solution to such problems—travelling to the still quiet place of the shadowless sun, through a portal to our higher or Good Mind. Only in the Good Mind, can we find our identity and restore our self-respect. Because most Native people live in both the Western and the Native world, I selected four cross-cultural tools to precipitate the time/space moment, which would springboard my students into an experience of the Good Mind. My instructional tools included:

- an identity Matrix;
- the Breath of Life Exercise;
- a Process for Reconciliation; and
- a Medicine Wheel – Immersion into the dimensions of the Good Mind.

Although Peck's model (see Chapter 6) would be my map, I needed a guide to help me with my first effort with an entire group of students. The Snow Owl became my guide because the owl had appeared to me, and because it offered the correct type of help. The Owl represents the power of the North to heal through a compassionate mind. Moreover, the Owl is considered a messenger between worlds—between night and day, between the spirit and everyday life.

Beginning the Process – "Who Are You?"

According to the traditional way of thinking, my task involved a four-step process:

1. to bond (and to bond with) a diverse group of people within a very short period time;

2. to help guide this group to place where their ancestors waited (My own people call this place *Yohts so non yahts tsiri yoh,* which means the Still Place and sheer joy, happiness, peacefulness, calm, and contentment—it is a known place.);

3. to facilitate their dialogue with this ancient identity (*Sah ni Kora Ahotoriso,* which means when you arrive at the Good Place, you're at harmony with the one you're speaking with.); and

4. to help my students return with new knowledge, which would empower their lives and their social work practice.

The first class was chaotic. Students came and went, scraping chairs and bumping tables. The sounds of snacking accompanied the general din of students visiting. It was clear that our program's standard course outline and introduction had not reached them! I wondered if Native process would.

I called for an opening ceremonial circle and invited everyone to participate. Only a handful responded. The others bunkered up in their chairs behind the tables to observe. Even then, the disruptive behavior continued. Their attitude shocked me because the circle is the fundamental belief in Native culture. Refusal to participate in a circle is tantamount to self-alienation. Acting on the assumption that loss, unexpressed grief, and pain were at the heart of this matter, I requested time alone with the students to process this pain in the dignity of Native company. My co-presenter, Kim Zapf, agreed and left the room.

First, I provided the students with additional information. I explained that social work practice recognized the importance of group process and that Native tradition does not endorse coercion. Therefore, students who did not want to participate in the smudge or the meditative part of the circle could remain outside the circle. However, after the smudge, participation in the circle was mandatory because both cultures require social workers who are competent in group discussion. The students moved slowly, but they complied.

To begin the discussion I asked "Who are you?" Most students gave me their English name; a few mentioned their tribes. I shared my encounter with Cyrus Peck and asked them why they had identified themselves as they had. At first they gave safe answers, "I didn't know what you wanted." But in a few minutes, other themes began to emerge: Residential school, no ceremonial background, and Christianity. At this point, I introduced my first instructional tool, the Identity Matrix.

1. Identity Matrix

	Family	Economics	Spiritual	Educational	Political
Traditional generation					
1					
2					
3					
4					
Non-traditional (western) generation					

Using the Identity Matrix

1. Explain that the purpose of this Matrix is to provide the student with a picture of his or her life. There is no good or bad, right or wrong to this exercise.

2. Then, either a traditional Elder or a Native instructor
   explains the concept of "Generations" (this term is best
   defined as both a verb and a noun). The Elder presents
   a verbal picture of the first or traditional generation and
   vividly describes what life was like before the invasion.
   (He or she covers all aspects on the horizontal axis.)

3. Students place an X beneath each category, according to
   the generation, that best describes their present
   "generations" or life.

Students usually discover that they are more traditional
than they thought they were and more Western than they
believed! Often they repeat this exercise to see where they
were in the past or to move their Xs to represent their goals.
Many questions emerge from this activity, which leads to the
next topic, "A History of Relations." This is a powerful and
emotive session. It should not be presented without traditional support. Instructors are advised to complete the
exercise for their own lives before introducing it to the class.
Western instructors will have to expand the Identity Matrix at
least seven generations in order to accommodate the
thousands of years of European detribalization.

2. The Breath of Life Exercise – Examining the Political Shaping of Native Communities

"You see, identity is something we have lost sight of and
were not told..."

The Identity Matrix provides a picture of life for an
individual, but Native people are tribal or communal; and
therefore, we get a community history. The community vision
is represented through the Tree of Life, because this Tree
represents perfect balance. Its roots sink deep into the Earth
to draw nutrients; its limbs extend upward to the Sun for
energy. The Tree breathes through its generations of leaves,
and as its seeds fall to the ground or rise from the roots, it
records its history in annual rings. The role of the Tree is vital
in ceremonies like the Sun Dance, which offers vision and
strength for community renewal.

By following the teachings of the Tree, we can look to the roots of our social problems. We look at history, and we look at the exchanges that occurred between Native societies and the dominant Western society. We continue the process of reaching for the sun because we want to regain balance in our lives. The Identity Matrix reveals the diffusion of the Native identity. Naturally, Native students want to know how and why this happened.

Most Western and Native relationships have been delineated by law—both from a tribe's Original (spiritual) instructions and from Western Domestic and International Laws. Therefore, "the History of Relations" looks at these two types of law as one way of organizing and making sense of a very complex and critical situation. The survival of today's Indian tribes depends on developing enlightened concepts of sovereignty. The History of Relations reveals the hidden events that have separated and divided these two cultures, and it sets the stage for their reconciliation and renewal.

The History of Relations

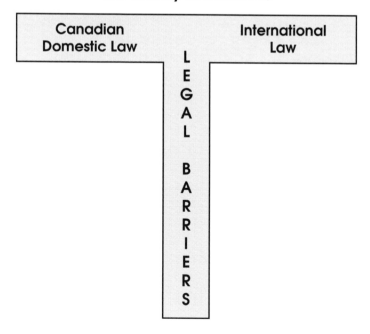

Canadian Domestic Law

The British North American Act (BNA) Act, 1867
- declares that commerce and trade with Indians are the province of Britain.
- is the first attempt to alter Native identity from natural, tribal units to the Western (linear and hierarchical) concept of "Nations"

Indian Act, 1876; Amended 1889, 1924, 1951
- tries to replace traditional Native government with Western elected government; bypasses elders and womens' counsels; the loyalties of paid, elected Native leaders are suspect.
- tries to define and determine membership by creating artificial Native "Nations." As a result, there are now at least five kinds of Indians including, Status, Non-Status, Treaty, Innuit, and Metis.

International Law

Before Contact:
- Good Mind
- Traditional government and natural communities (not nations)

After Contact:
- Treaties
- World Court
- United Nations

Explanation

Prior to colonization, Native societies were organized by bio-regional, linguistic kinship systems. The names for these biologically-based expressions of intelligence included Dene and Cree. These societies, which connected all Native people with the universe, moved through large family systems. Their government was based on balance and renewal. Their leaders were selected by the Elders, who carefully watched these individuals grow and develop. There was no concept of "nation" or "nation state." The people lived in accordance with the laws of life, which were given to each person at birth. As a first step in expropriating Native lands, European government imposed the word "Nation" on original tribal names.

Native peoples had to become Nation States in order to hold legal title to their lands.

In the early days of contact, the vast number of Natives forced the European nations to enter into treaties in order to secure their political and economic interests. These treaties were, and still remain, within the purview of International Law. Native social workers and social work instructors must understand the significance of these treaties because they are the international guarantees of Native lands and human rights. These treaties also provide the legal basis for the funding of Native social work education programs and Band social services.

International Law recognizes the legal barriers that exist between nations. The law requires that Canada (or any colonial government) must prove its right to take Indian lands. The taking of Native lands must then satisfy one of three legal tests: The Law of Discovery, the Law of War, or the Law of Cession. The crisis precipitated by presenting this kind of information can open the doors to a new, healthier, and more equitable relationship between both Western and Native peoples.

As students consider this material, they begin to see contradictions and to ask questions that help to clarify values, affirm identity, and create a healthier foundation for cross-cultural relationships. The following questions are common:

- *If Canada is trying to educate, improve, and uplift Native life, why are laws like the Indian Act enforced?*

Discussion: Introduce the concepts of overt and latent political policy objectives. This information helps depersonalise blame and allows creative strategies to emerge.

- *What is the real government of Native people?*

Discussion: Highlight traditional forms of Native government such as the spiritual Constitution of a tribe's origin and identity and the biological, social kinship forms of traditional government. Clarify and affirm the traditional, spiritual, and biological forms of tribal governance, including ecological teachings and democratic principles. This discussion will also establish the strong position of traditional Elders, Clan Mothers, Uncles, and Aunts in Native society.

- *How can elected government officials serve the Native people if they are being paid by Ottawa?*

Discussion: The resolution may lie in the renewed (or rediscovered) commitment to the consciousness of the Good Mind or the authentic Native Mind. Ask students to provide the local terms for Good Mind (*Kin De hucho* – Dene or *Meyo man to need chik eet* – Cree). Examine the similarities and differences between the Good Mind and the assimilated mind. Look at the consequences of each on a tribal, personal, family, and cross-cultural level. Through this discussion, people can begin to make conscious choices. One student used these ideas as a point of discussion with her Chief and was subsequently invited to make a presentation to the entire Council!

These are questions that all informed citizens ought to ask of their government. But Native people are seldom encouraged to look to the roots of their social problems, and they are often prevented from developing a critical conscious-ness. Deep seated cross-cultural fears, guilt, and antagonisms seem to lie at the heart of the matter. When these emotions, are examined, they can be used to shift us into a more creative mode. I developed the "Colonization of the Mind" to help trigger this shift. This model will raise complex questions and provoke strong feelings. Therefore, it is essential that several positive alternatives be explored as a follow-up to this procedure.

3. A Process for Reconciliation – Colonization, the Psychological Shaping of the Native Mind

"You were not told by your mother or father because they were discouraged..."

In his book, *The Peculiar Institution,* Kenneth Stamp examined the records of slave owners in the Southern United States. To help students understand how the history of Native colonization has affected our Good Mind, I have summarised the results of Stamp's investigations:

1. Establish and maintain strict discipline with unconditional submission. The Native is never allowed to exercise either his will or judgement in opposition to a positive order.

2. Inculcate the Native with a consciousness of personal inferiority. They are to know and keep their place and to feel the difference between the White man and the Indian. They must feel that ancestry taints and that colour is a badge of degradation.

3. Awe them with a sense of the White man's enormous power couched within the principle of fear.

4. Persuade the Native to take an interest in the White man's enterprise and to accept his standards of good conduct. The colonizer must show the Indians that the advancement of his interests are the same as the advancement of theirs. Once they feel this, it will take little effort to make them act as required.

To process this material, I used Peck's question, "Finally, come to the point. Why are you like this when your great uncles are self-respecting people?" Students are able to answer this question for the first time in their lives. It is an overwhelming experience of grief and forgiveness of self and community. It provides them with the opening to ask for help in finding their identity.

Memories of residential school abuse, the indifference of Indian Affairs agents and their interference in Band life, alcoholism, physical abuse, and many other outcomes of genocide are identified and externalised. Although this exercise may begin as a theoretical discussion, its serious tone requires a safe space for disclosure. Therefore, it is best to move into Circle, because there, the rules of confidentiality, no cross-talk, and the right to speak apply. Western instructors **should not** undertake this exercise without the support of a traditional Native person who has proper training and a personal history! Agencies that have strict traditional and Western standards, such as the Nechi Institute, can be useful resources.

A word of caution. This exercise elicits strong feelings of anger against the abuses of Western society. There is a danger that this rage can become racial and turned against White people. Two pieces of information can keep this process positive. First, the students must be introduced to the tribal background of Europe, and Western instructors must present their own tribal histories. The process that destroyed much of Native life was the same process that was used against most of the tribes of Europe. Second, the instructor must present evidence of the much longer period of positive relations between Western and Native people (largely in pre-history) as well as examples of exceptional Europeans who rose above prevailing ideology to embrace Native life. John Collier, the first social scientist to head the Department of Indian Affairs in the United States was one such person; there are many others.

In itself, this information will not be sufficient to bridge the historical distrust. Only humility and compassion will serve. Western instructors must be able to enter into the reality of Native students. They must feel and express regret for what Westerners have done; they must honestly experience and share the loss of their ancestral European lands, ways, and connections. In the mutuality of this moment, true reconciliation occurs. Virginia Satir, who has worked extensively to reconstruct the Native family, once told me, "I may not be responsible for what has happened in the past, but I'm making myself responsible for what happens now!"

Students will need a few days to process this knowledge with their family and friends. When the class reconvenes, it is important to hold a circle to share the experiences of this new identity. When the group comes to closure, the instructor introduces the last part of the journey, the Good Mind. The Good Mind is the highest level of consciousness and the deepest psychological level of self.

4. A Medicine Wheel – Immersion into the Dimensions of the Good Mind

"Self Respect goes back a long ways, that's the way we have been created..."

The moment that a person asks, "who am I?" Cyrus Peck introduces information and then returns to his original question, "Who are You?" The Snow Owl Process introduces the concept of the Good Mind to help students answer that essential question. The Good Mind exists in all Native cultures, although each has a different term to describe it. It is the organizing spirit of Native life; it is both process and structure; it is the place to which we have always travelled in search of identity and meaning. It is the sacred meeting place between worlds. In the Snow Owl Process, we search for the ancient, authentic Native mind. As we do so, we are wonderfully aware that we are following in the footsteps of our ancestors.

As we travel, bits and pieces of genetically and culturally encoded information begin to surface. Scraps of a story, a piece of a song, chant, or technique come to mind and direct our footsteps. For Native people who have been told, and have believed, that they know nothing or have nothing of value, being united with the life of the people is sheer joy. We become one with ourselves and with our ancestors. We are transformed.

To prepare the students for this journey, review the local terms for the Good Mind. Then discuss examples and experiences of this mind such as lucid dreams, powerful encounters with animals, moments of prescience, the conception of a child, an old person's presence, and the love of a child. Discuss the good, strong feelings that these experiences impart and share stories of Elders who live in this state of mind.

A common understanding of the nature of, and a feeling for, the Good Mind begins to emerge in the group. This generalized understanding must be brought into the conscious mind so that the students can find and travel to this place whenever they wish. Traditionally, Native people have used prayer sticks or Medicine Wheels to help them find *axis mundi* or the Good Mind. Because Alberta has the greatest number of Medicine Wheels (ancient rock structures) in North America, I relied on the Wheel to present the basic concepts.

The sacred directions are the most basic information on the Medicine Wheel. Each direction represents an energy and an intelligence with which we can communicate. They are not merely symbolic; these directions are real.

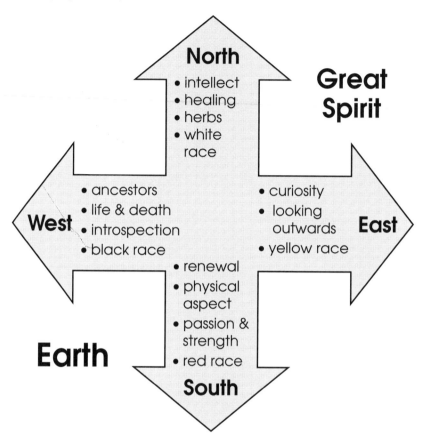

The Medicine Wheel is life, and it explains how various aspects of life fit together. Accommodation to life is so important to Native people that when the Iroquois say "Hello," they are actually asking, "The Good Mind, are you with it/in it?" The Wheel contains the colours, sounds, plants, animals, stories, and stars that belong to each direction. As we learn about each of these aspects of life, we are better able to communicate with and to receive instruction from the Wheel. The Directions become more real, and we see how they work to keep life in balance. For example, if I am too deeply involved with the Northern intellectual aspect of my life, troubles will manifest themselves in the Southern physical or family health side of my life. If I look too hard for meaning outside of myself, in an Easterly direction, some difficulty is certain to make me look within myself, in a Westerly direction.

When we begin to see how the circle of life works, we realize that we are not alone, that we can regain our identity and our self-respect. Eventually, we see the goodness of life and realize that each day is a gift. We sense the enormous, unconditional love behind this realization. In that moment, when we are thankful, we enter into our Good Mind.

Conclusion

In this chapter, I have presented the Snow Owl Process as a linear sequence. I used the four tools in the order presented; however, throughout the course of our study we practised the process even before we learned it. Each day began with a Circle and a smudge; rituals that teach holism were used at every opportunity. By the time the students were introduced to the Wheel, they had practised reaching the Good Mind many times. The only difference is that now they can go there consciously.

I began this article by talking about the shadowless sun, the collapsed sense of time and space that Native people enjoy. I mentioned nearly hitting a Native man on the highway and then seeing the Snow Owl. How do these things fit together? The Good Mind teaches us to see the balance. Something of Great Power will always be balanced by a Sacred Clown or a difficulty. One sets the stage for the other. Interestingly, we looked for this same man on our return trip to town. He was nowhere to be seen.

When we look at the relationship between the Western and the Native peoples, we see a great imbalance. This imbalance was created by linear thought, which emphasizes separation and hierarchy. It also gives rise to science and technology, which shape the mind so powerfully that Western-thinking people often confuse linearity with reality. The late esteemed physicist, David Bohm, pointed out that science has fallen prey to its own propaganda. Since Einstein, the West has been aware that a particle is also a wave and that an observer shapes what he or she sees. Yet science, which leads Western thought, continues to operate on pre-Einsteinian understandings. Such rationality leads to global insanity.

For a brief moment, in a classroom in the far North, a group of Native social work students left the confines of linear thought behind and discovered a whole mind. The process they used is described here for those who wish to follow. If Native thinking is correct, not being controlled by a false, linear view of reality is a harbinger to a powerful, life-enhancing transformation. The secret is to find the way to the meeting place of our true, Good Mind. This is power of the Owl, the Gift of the North.

Have you ever visited the home ground of owls? Try it. Stand in the mystery of your own life.

References

Colorado, P. (1985). *Native American alcoholism: An issue of survival*. Doctoral dissertation. Boston, MA: Brandeis University.

Colorado, P. (1985). *Voices upon the water*. Sitka, AL: Southeast Alaska Regional Training Program.

Bastien, B., Colorado, P., et al (1987). *Indian Association of Alberta child welfare needs assessment and recommendations*. Edmonton, AB:

Colorado, P. (1992). *A Native view of development, conflicts of interest, Canada and the Third World*.

Deloria, V. (1986). *Power and place equal personality, winds of change*. Boulder, CO: American Indigeous Science & Engineering.

Frideres, J.S. (1983). *Native People in Canada: Contemporary conflicts* (2nd ed.). Scarborough, ON: Prentice-Hall.

Stampp, K. (1989). *Peculiar institution*. New York, NY: Random House.

Traditional Support provided by:
Sydney Stone Brown, Blackfoot, Portland, Oregon. Developed a pre-self actualization matrix (circa 1980) which I have adapted and expanded for use in the Snow Owl Process.

Woodrow Morrison, Jr. J.D., Haida, Hydaburg, Alaska. Conceived a framework for contrasting domestic and international law, which I have expanded with the Good Mind and the sacred "T."

Chapter 8

Methods Instruction as a Two-way Process

Michael Kim Zapf

Native outreach education in social work is a relatively new endeavour. Although our current knowledge base cannot support rigorous research designs, we are obviously in an important exploratory stage. Numerous college and university social work schools are delivering outreach programs onsite in Native communities. The experiences of those instructors, students, and communities must be recorded and considered if we expect to develop more effective and appropriate outreach programs.

This chapter describes my experiences and some of the insights I gained while working as a sessional instructor for Grant MacEwan Community College teaching two outreach social work methods courses to a group of Native students. Let me briefly introduce myself and the setting in order to provide a background for the discussion that follows. I am a white male academic who has social work experience across northern Canada. At present, I am a member of The

University of Calgary Faculty of Social Work where my research and teaching focuses on practice in rural and northern communities. The setting for the particular social work methods courses I taught for Grant MacEwan Community College was High Level, Alberta, a small community about 800 kilometres north of Edmonton and 200 kilometres south of the Northwest Territories border. (I can assure you that both High Level and the author are more animated than these thumbnail introductions convey!)

In presenting this material, I have deliberately chosen to write in the first rather than the third person voice because the conclusions I offer are based on my immediate experience. I am not reporting the results of a rigorous empirical design. Although I can claim no external validity for my conclusions in research terms, my experiences in High Level had an unanticipated and profound impact on my understanding of my role as a teacher and a learner in Native outreach education. Through the use of anecdotes and specific material from those courses, I hope to convey some of the power and the challenge of that experience as the starting point for proposing that methods instruction can be a two-way process.

The First Methods Course

In the fall of 1991, I was contracted to be an instructor for the *Social Work Practice Methods I* course offered to a class of Native students in High Level, Alberta. The course outline I was given in Edmonton included many handouts and assigned readings from standard social work methods textbooks. As with most methods courses, the course grade was based largely on written assignments and the submission of a taped interview with transcript and analysis. The social work program in High Level involved twenty students, and for this course the class was divided into two sections. The instructor of the other section was also non-Native and from Edmonton where she worked as a full-time faculty member with the Grant MacEwan College Social Work Program. I often relied on her for direction as she had previous experience teaching this particular course in other settings.

I learned that the usual number of instructional hours reserved for this course had been doubled for the High Level students. A 45-hour course in Edmonton, the *Social Work Practice Methods I* course in High Level was scheduled as 90 hours. I learned that there were two main reasons for the additional hours:

- compared with the urban campus group in Edmonton, students in High Level had some educational deficits; and

- many of the High Level students would have personal experience as victims of the social problems examined in class and may require class time to work through some of their unresolved issues.

In our case, the 90 course hours were divided into 15 instruction days of six hours each. Over a period of three months, we flew to High Level five times, each time for three days, to deliver the *Methods I* course.

After the first few classes, it became readily apparent that the students were not familiar with the material from their assigned readings. When I identified this as an issue in class, I discovered that many of the students had extensive community and family commitments outside of class. All of the students except one were women; in addition to being students, most had responsibilities as mothers, partners, and homemakers. For them, uninterrupted quiet time for reading and concentration did not exist outside of the school. A second problem appeared as I talked with the students who were actually doing the readings as assigned but seemed quite unaware of what they had read. They were not careless or lazy students. Often they spent long hours reading the assigned material but it just did not connect. Their previous experiences with formal education taught them to read a text looking for the "answers" or for points or lists they might expect to be on an exam. This methods course was asking them to connect the readings with their personal experiences in order to develop their own analytical skills; however, the examples provided in the text were foreign to their situation in High Level.

Michael Kim Zapf

In an attempt to address these problems, a portion of each class was devoted to reading. This activity appeared to be an appropriate use of the extra hours; it provided a quiet focused reading opportunity with no distractions. Often one student would read aloud while the rest of the group followed in their text. After each paragraph, we would stop and discuss the material. I diligently searched for examples, parallels, and connections that would reflect the students' experiences.

The written exams were administered in an open-book format to avoid receiving responses of memorized lists of irrelevant material. Instead, the students were given case examples and asked to discuss them using the models from the book and their own experiences. Considerable class time was also allocated for work on the required taped interview, plus transcript and analysis. During these sessions, the class operated as an open workshop. Students learned from each other's questions and progress on their assignments while I acted as tutor.

At the end of the *Social Work Practice Methods I* course, I did not experience the usual sense of satisfaction I have when a contract is completed. All of the students had demonstrated basic interviewing skills at an acceptable level and were beginning to grasp the process of generalist practice; all had passed the course, with a few doing very well. Yet I had an uncomfortable feeling that we had missed something. We had not taken full advantage of the opportunity presented to us during our time together.

I had spent the full 90 hours teaching, leading skills exercises, reading in class, tutoring workshops on assignments, and dealing with personal issues raised in class. Because I had been expecting student deficits, I had certainly found them. It was a clear case of self-fulfilling prophecy. I had helped students with reading, with speaking in class, and with organizing essay and assignment materials. Yet all of this work was bringing them into my realm, my world, my Western mind set.

I began to reflect on evidence of another reality which I had missed or ignored during the period of this course. I recalled how students who were very quiet in class became animated and boisterous during breaks, and conversed freely in their own language within their own family groupings. Many who had difficulty mastering the basic skills in class had been working in social service positions in this district for years. Several were already well known as helpers and respected resource persons in their own communities. Because the methods course had been a one-way process, few of their strengths had been revealed in class. I had learned very little about their community and almost nothing about their helping approach.

I had done everything I could to teach these students my approach. We had worked hard together on overcoming the obstacles that prevented them from demonstrating Western skills, focused on problems that are defined from a Western perspective, in order for them to receive a satisfactory Western grade. Using a popular metaphor from cross-cultural counselling, I began to see how this one-way process had successfully pulled the students closer to my side, but it did nothing to build a bridge that might be useful for us both. Mainstream methods textbooks and conventional course outlines even support this one-way approach by using labels such as "holistic" and "generic" which disguise the cultural assumptions and mind-set in which the model is rooted.

I had faithfully delivered course content in a forum where I was the acknowledged expert, and where the students by definition had deficits or obstacles to overcome. I may have done an excellent job adapting and presenting the material but I had risked nothing of myself. I had learned very little, and I may even have contributed to the devaluation of the students' strengths and identities. Fortunately, I had an opportunity to move beyond this experience and try things differently in the second methods course.

The Second Methods Course

With all of these uncomfortable and unresolved issues remaining, I approached the second methods course in High Level in the winter of 1992 with a little more humility and respect for the task ahead. Could the reality and traditions of the students be integrated into the classroom encounter?

The course outline for *Social Work Practice Methods II* from Grant MacEwan Community College specifies that

> the course will unite the social work/communication skills learned in Methods I with the process of help based on an ecological systems perspective.

From the outset, I began to see the dangerous one-way assumptions. What could my system, my Western scientific tradition, teach Native people about an "ecological systems perspective"? While the western mind is dealing conceptually with whole systems thinking, aboriginal communities around the world have been living holistically. I considered that I might learn something about an ecological approach in High Level if I adjusted my mind set. The most exciting thought was that perhaps the entire course could incorporate such a two-way learning process.

The instructor hired to teach the other section of *Methods II* was Dr. Pam Colorado. A Native woman with a PhD in social work, Dr. Colorado is a powerful healer in the Native tradition as well as an accomplished academic and practitioner in the Western school. During the course, Dr. Colorado asked her students and colleagues to call her by her Indian name, Apela. I will use that name when I refer to her throughout this discussion of the events in High Level.

Although Apela and I had worked together in other areas and had taught in the same program on several occasions, we had never actually been in the same classroom together. We decided on a different approach for this course in High Level. Rather than split the class into two sections and assign an instructor to each section, we would combine the sections and teach together. This approach would give the students both a Native and a western perspective in the classroom at the same time. Material could be presented by one instructor and then critiqued by the other. The 90 hours of *Social Work Practice Methods II* were scheduled into three one-week blocks which would give both the instructors and the students time to concentrate on their challenging tasks. The week-long sessions in High Level gave Apela and me time together to plan, to reflect, and to assess our progress before each day's long session.

The students responded very well to this approach. Some described how they "flipped" between their Indian mind and their Western mind. Having Apela and me as models for these "mindflips" encouraged students to participate in the work. They watched us sort out the differences and similarities between our two approaches, which was sometimes painful and sometimes very funny, in an atmosphere of trust and support.

Students told us they had previously been left to do this integration on their own. Native content had been presented by Native resource people when possible; Western content had usually been presented by non-Native instructors. The students had become quite adept at producing what was needed to pass a course with either their Indian mind or their Western mind. Because the two minds seldom came together in the classroom, however, students often felt split. The result was a lack of confidence in gaining proficiency in either system. Having students watch and then participate as we explored these connections in the classroom was a profound learning experience for them and for us.

Each day began in a ceremonial manner with a circle for smudge, prayer, and affirmations. The first few days, Apela led the ceremonies and taught about the circle, the directions, and respect for each other. Later, students assumed the various functions in the circle. In many ways, this tradition prepared us for our day's work. We dealt with many issues in the circle: the unfinished business from the previous day; overnight reflections and insights on our work; personal accounts of the fear, the pain, and the humour associated with our work; affirmations of the importance of our work and the value of each other. Gratitude was often expressed for the progress we were making, and appeals were made for guidance with the tasks ahead. When we were ready, we moved out of the circle and began working. Most days the circle session took about half an hour; some days much more time was needed.

Images From the Work

I cannot describe a typical day because each day was different. Although we ensured that required content areas were addressed, the instructional approaches we used were innovative responses to what was going on in class. We could not have predicted or prescribed our activities in a course outline. I would like to present several brief scenarios, a few frozen highlights or images, that may illustrate the excitement and the impact of the two-way learning process that occurred during the course.

The first scene describes the point at which the students and the instructors realized that we were committing ourselves to a new and risky two-way process of learning.

Early in the course, Apela spent a half-day with the students exploring the impact of internalized colonization. She reviewed the history and process of colonization, then guided the students through experiential exercises to discover the ongoing internalized thought processes that continue the victimization and personal devaluation. Students reached for their own pain and anger at this devastating legacy on their communities, their families, and their own identities.

This experiential component, the intense grief and anger that must be recognized and confronted, is something that Apela has worked on herself for many years. She could share her own struggles with her Native students and guide them into the process. However, she did not feel comfortable doing this activity with a non-Native present; I respected her judgment and stayed away.

The next morning was extremely difficult. The experience of the previous day had been profound. Many students had spent the night agonizing over the buried issues that had now been made conscious. Not only was I the only non-Native in the room, now I was also a white male authority figure, an easy target. Many students avoided eye contact with me. Some refused to join the circle if I was there. Some students gave voice to their anger, and questioned my motives and my right to be there at all.

It was very hard to take. I felt betrayed and resentful that I had been used as a target. What had happened to our nice little class? With Apela's support, I moved past my initial defensive reactions. I could see that it was not a personal attack; the students simply needed a target for their new rage. How I reacted would be crucial for our future work together. If I retreated to the safety of the instructor/student relationship, or used the trite defence that I had not personally harmed anyone, I would be perpetuating the colonial process. They were experiencing and experimenting with powerful new and frightening feelings, and looking at some of the real problems that exist between our cultures.

I acknowledged my initial defensive feelings. I told them that the colonial process had been internalized by the colonizers as well as the victims. I had much to unlearn and relearn about my past and my assumptions. I shared my personal discoveries, from early images of Tonto and Injun Joe through to the northern Native communities in which I had worked.

*It was a slow and difficult sharing process, with hesitation and tears on both sides. I was involved with this class, and with **our** process, with an immediacy I had never experienced through prepared lectures, lab exercises, or class discussions. This process moved beyond instructor/student. We were risking and listening, learning about each other's tasks. For them, the dominant feeling was anger; for me, it was guilt. Enough trust had been established so that we allowed ourselves to be each other's targets.*

*We came to the following realization, probably the most powerful and crucial insight to come out of the course: **If their anger forced them to shut me out and dismiss me, or if my guilt sent me back to the city where I could comfortably ignore the issue, then a special opportunity to build a bridge that we both needed would be wasted.***

We agreed to stay with the struggle with our new understanding of each other's tasks and the feelings involved. From this point on, the learning was indeed a two-way process.

The next scenario illustrates the bridging process that can occur when both western and Native minds are free to question each other's assumptions and even their language.

I had just finished summarizing the stages of the generalist model. There on the blackboard were the labels:

Initial Contact, Engagement, Assessment, Implementa-
tion, Termination. Students had been busy copying down the
terms and making notes from my comments on each stage.
William, the program coordinator, seemed very troubled.
"Aren't those the same stages" he asked, "as the colonization
process?" An awkward silence followed as the impact of his
insight hit. Of course the sequence was the same!

This sequential approach to planned change could be used
for exploitation as well as helping. It was a process that
depended upon the values and awareness of the people who
used the approach. The class discussed how a Hitler or a
colonizer or a developer could effectively use the same model.

One student asked how we could expect her to take this
model into her community to help when this very approach had
caused so much suffering and oppression in the past. We spent
a long time exploring this question. The model itself was not
destructive. Although it was potentially powerful in terms of
impact, it was relatively neutral in terms of values. The process
itself did not actually oppose traditional Native approaches to
helping, but it was regarded with suspicion and some fear
because of its terrible history. We discovered that even the
language was getting in the way. When we replaced
"assessment, implementation, and termination" with "vision
and transformation," the process fit much better with local
conditions and traditional approaches to helping.

Course content was not the only thing our two-way
learning process affected. The relationship between instructor
and student changes profoundly when both are perceived as
teacher and learner with parallel tasks. In the next scenario,
consider how the role of one particular student changed in this
course, as well as my role as her teacher.

Prior to the first Methods course, I was informed that one
of the women in the class was older than the others. In fact, she
was a grandmother. I was told that she was quiet but
determined, someone who would work hard to complete the
program, but would not say much in class, and someone who
could have trouble with the reading and written work. Of
course, I found these "deficits" because I was looking for them.

My limitations prevented me from seeing this woman's strengths and learning from her during that first course.

Early in the Methods II course, Apela told me that she sensed a great power from this student. She suggested that this woman's perspective as an Elder and a grandmother could be very helpful for us and the class. Apela thought we should approach her in a traditional way and ask for her help with our work. Apela would bring tobacco and I was to bring a scarf. We would offer these gifts to the elder in the circle and ask for her help.

This plan scared me on many levels. In my system, it is not acceptable for an instructor to offer a gift to a student, especially in front of other students. What if the students think I have selected a favourite? What if someone appeals? I have enough trouble choosing a gift for my own grandmother, let alone select a scarf for a woman about whom I know very little. What if I make a bad selection? What if I offend her? What if she thinks I'm silly, or making fun of her?

Apela explained the gifts in terms of balance; they were offered in exchange for the help we were requesting. She taught me of the importance of cloth and its connections with the earth and with dancing. Rather than some designer silk creation, she suggested I seek a cotton scarf with a simple design. But it was important that I select it.

When the moment finally came, Apela invited the woman and me into the circle. I had the scarf but I was still very nervous that I would make some major mistake and either offend her, or look foolish, or both. Do I enter the circle first, or do I wait and follow her? Do women enter before men? Does an Elder enter last? Once inside, do we sit? Do I sit first, or do I wait for her? Will she expect me to speak first, or do I wait for her to speak? There were a million ways I could screw this up in front of everybody.

Once we sat and this grandmother held my hand, all of these fears disappeared. I relaxed, feeling not only very comfortable but also very secure with her. She knew I was trying my best to approach her in a respectful way and that we really wanted and needed her help. She agreed to help us with our work in the class.

This woman became an important leader and resource person throughout the rest of the course. For example, when the students were working in small groups developing case study assessments and work plans, the grandmother, Apela, and I would move from group to group offering advice and answering questions based on our own experiences and perspectives.

Throughout this process, I became increasingly aware of how little I really knew about traditional Native helping approaches. The next scenario provides a glimpse of my learning process.

We began to conduct role-play interviews, much as we had done in the previous methods course. However, in this course, Apela would conduct an interview using a traditional Indian approach while I would use a Western approach. Students could watch and comment on either approach or get involved and participate with either model.

I watched Apela conduct interviews with very few words and, sometimes, complete silence. I began to understand how limited my understanding of this process was. I had learned and practiced the conventional simplistic list of "tips for interviewing Natives," things such as limited eye contact, comfort with silence, nonintrusiveness, and avoiding direct questions. But I was seeing something more here. Apela was not just avoiding or delaying dialogue; she and her client were waiting for something. As she explained later, they were "waiting for the spirit to show itself."

To help me understand, she gave me an image. In her language, the "Giilai" is that deep pool at the top of a waterfall where tired salmon can find peace in calm water full of nutrients before resuming their struggle upstream. When two people reach that level of peace, or speak from the "Giilai," a profound connection is possible. Until they reach it, they may be wise to wait or do something else.

That image of the "Giilai" has haunted me ever since. Often, as now I prepare for meetings, interviews, and even time with family, I realize how my culture places the clock ahead of readiness. I must begin when it is time to begin regardless of my inner state. Although I try to begin "where the client is at" emotionally, intellectually, and socially, I seldom consider my client's inner peace or how to facilitate it, or wait for it trusting that it will come. The students in this course laughed as they saw me struggle to set aside my Western mind and not view the schedule as paramount. It is difficult for me to wait and trust; my Western helping models all focus on action.

Through these encounters with Native helping approaches, I came to see clearly how my Western system has removed the spirit from the helping process. As a Westerner, I operate on a linear system of time with a past that strongly influences the present. My profession concentrates on instigating planned change and mobilizing resources toward some desired goal for the future. As I learned more about a circular view of time from Apela and the Native students, I began to sense the importance of ancestors and future generations in the Native helping process. Although my Western system trumpets an ecological approach to social and physical environments, we want our spirits to remain linear. A circular notion of time allows for spirits to be involved with the helping process.

Obviously, I cannot write authoritatively about Native spirituality. I cannot explain how it works or how to use it. Even my language reflects the limitations of my Western approach as I have isolated spirituality as some sort of special technique. Nevertheless, I was privileged to watch Native helpers effectively use forces that are not well known or understood in my Western system. Once again, I became aware of limitations in the models I teach as generic and holistic. The last scenario describes how we were able to explore this sensitive area in the trusting atmosphere we had created.

A candle was lit in the centre of the circle. As one of the students spoke from her heart on a very difficult issue, the flame began to behave very strangely, and the smoke made a sudden and dramatic shift in direction. The student recognized this movement as the spiritual presence of a deceased relative.

After we left the circle, I told the students I wanted to share something with them that would illustrate some dangers of the

Western approach to knowing. I cautioned them that they might be disturbed by what I was about to say. They agreed and I began.

I told them that as a Western scientist I could not accept all this hocus-pocus about the presence of a spirit in the circle based on one observation in a situation with so many uncontrolled variables. Next time we would use several candles to ensure that the effect was not due to some defect in the wick. We would also tape all of the windows and doors to control drafts. Then the student would call on the spirit at times randomly selected by me. If all these things were done and the manifestation still occurred each time, then I would have strong evidence of a spiritual presence.

Initial suspicion and anger soon turned to laughter. Obviously my Western approach would prevent me from ever experiencing this type of presence again. My sceptical Western mind and empirical approach to learning fails me in such situations.

Conclusion

Based on my experiences with the methods courses in High Level, I can offer some suggestions that might be useful to other non-Native instructors, inferences I have drawn from talking about and reflecting on the events that occurred in High Level. This chapter is not a prescription for how to teach social work methods to Native students, and it is not a package to be delivered in other Native communities. Although I could not recreate the High Level experiences at will in other courses, I can work to promote a two-way learning process with Native students. In that spirit, I offer four guidelines which may prove useful to other instructors:

- **Seek out opportunities to co-teach with a Native instructor.** This partnership will require personal commitments of time and sharing as you work to develop a relationship of trust. In turn, this relationship will allow you to model for your class the struggles involved in building connections between your two belief systems.

Co-teaching opportunities are rare at the present time because there are only a few Native social work educators in our system. You may have to seek the help of known local natural helpers who are qualified and respected in their community. You should also encourage your institution to recruit and actively support Native faculty.

- **Be humble.** Although you are hired to teach these courses on the basis of your expertise and credentials, you will be a guest in the community and assessed as a person not just an instructor. Acknowledging the limitations of your approach is the first step towards encouraging a two-way learning process.

- **Prepare yourself.** This is not just a trite reminder to bring all your handouts and a spare pen. Preparing to teach social work courses in Native communities involves a major commitment. Most of us have to begin with a process Collier (1984) describes as "unlearning" or Wharf (1985) calls "reframing."

> Many of us learned in public school about the Europeans' *discovery* of North America, about brave explorers surviving on their own ingenuity in a harsh and empty land, about Indian *massacres,* about dedicated missionaries saving heathen souls, about determined settlers carving a new life out of the wilderness. These events need to be reconsidered from the perspective of exploitation, underdevelopment, and colonialism. The underlying ideologies of racism, sexism, and capitalism may have been rendered invisible in our early schooling.
>
> Zapf, 1992, (p. 43–44.)

As more of us start on this journey, we are fortunate that a new literature is developing to guide us. Begin reading and discuss some of these ideas with Native friends and colleagues. I found the following books to be particularly helpful: *Mother Earth Spirituality* (McGaa, 1990), *Rainbow Tribe* (McGaa, 1992), *Stolen Continents* (Wright, 1991), *Occupied Canada* (Hunter and Calihoo, 1991), and *A Long and Terrible Shadow* (Berger, 1991).

- **Record your experiences.** We must learn from each other and build a solid knowledge base for outreach social work education in Native communities. Because it has a strong subjective component, the two-way learning process can be more difficult to write about than conventional academic subjects. You will be writing about experiences that you may not be able to adequately describe. You risk the judgment of those who would dismiss your experiences. Yet your efforts are important. After all, Native students have the courage to risk this vulnerability every day in your class when they have to "flip" to their Western minds.

References

Berger, T.A. (1991). *A Long and terrible shadow: White values & Native rights in the Americas 1492–1992*. Vancouver: Douglas & McIntyre.

Collier, K. (1984). *Social work with rural peoples: Theory and practice*. Vancouver: New Star.

Hunter, R., & Calihoo, R. (1991). *Occupied Canada: A young white man discovers his unsuspected past*. Toronto: McClelland & Stewart.

McGaa, E. (Eagle Man). (1990). *Mother Earth spirituality: Native American paths to healing ourselves and our world*. New York: Harper Collins.

McGaa, E. (Eagle Man). (1992). *Rainbow tribe: Ordinary people journey on the Red road*. New York: Harper Collins.

Wharf, B. (1985). Toward a leadership role in human services: The case for rural communities. *The Social Worker, 53*(1), 14–20.

Wright, R. (1991). *Stolen continents: The new world through Indian eyes since 1492*. Toronto: Viking.

Zapf, M.K. (1992). Educating social work practitioners for the north: A challenge for conventional models and structures. *The Northern Review, 7*, 35–52.

Chapter 9

A 'Grand Lady's' Voyage into Nowhere Land

Sophie Freud

Seizing the Day

In December, 1985, I reluctantly agreed to participate in a media event called *The Evolution of Psychotherapy,* which took place in Phoenix, Arizona. Kay Feehan, Chair, of the Social Work Program at Grant MacEwan Community College in Edmonton, Alberta attended my presentation and later invited me to participate in their faculty colloquium in Edmonton the following October. I flourished in their friendly reception and enjoyed meeting with their faculty members and students. During this visit, I overheard several faculty members discussing their "Outreach Programs." These programs were designed to give rural and Native students an opportunity to further their social work education and provide trained staff for the local human services agencies.

After living in Boston for many years, this was just the kind of "peace-corps" type of teaching I had been yearning to do. Too bad that I was getting too old for such adventures. Six months later, as I was making plans for my second sabbatical, a whisper from my personal guardian angel persuaded me to forget my age and suggested I ask if I could spend a semester in such an instructional setting. I will not dwell here on how much it meant to have my tentative offer accepted with such warmth and enthusiasm by Kay Feehan and the people at Grant MacEwan Community College. I hope that the description of my teaching experiences in the Social Work Outreach program also expresses my gratitude to all the people who helped make this unique life experience possible for me.

This series of events, where one opportunity leads to other more important ones, has served to reinforce my "opportunity theory." Each life is touched by opportunities, which may either be wholeheartedly embraced or completely rejected, or perhaps, go completely unnoticed. As teachers and counsellors, we can encourage our students and clients to be aware, and to take advantage of opportunities that cross their paths—opportunities that may make the difference between leading a rich or an impoverished life. Fortunately, I was able to seize the day.

It has been my habit to "nail down the events of my life" by writing a detailed diary. I needed to capture the experience of "teaching in Grouard" before it disappeared like a dream. I am taking this *opportunity* to share with you a part of the diary I wrote during that time. However, I have made some changes to the original text. I have converted the present tense to the past, changed the names of the individuals involved, collapsed the personalities of many students into a few representative cases, and disguised various identifying details. I have regretfully refrained from including most of the vivid, and often traumatic, stories my students told me about their lives. Although these stories would provide readers with a more lively picture of these resilient people, I was obligated to protect their privacy and remain focused on our teaching experience. I hope that any students who think that they may recognize themselves, or perhaps pieces of themselves, will smile forgivingly as they reminisce with me.

Getting Started

"Your eyelids will freeze shut and you will never be able to open your eyes again," said my son in a sternly protective voice to his aging mother. "Why go half way up to the North Pole?" Many people asked similar questions. Reasons always seem to come and go, and if we need an explanation for our behavior, we can simply choose the one that suits us best at a particular moment. For example, I went to Grouard, Alberta to hide, to rest, to read the books I never had time to read, to make a difference, and to seek the unusual. (Later, I would favor another explanation, because I did not achieve most of these goals.)

Basically, I am a teacher, and in this capacity, I seek new challenges and opportunities. That was my favorite explanation as to why I went to Grouard to teach *Methods II,* which I had never taught systematically, and *Group Work,* which I had never taught in quite that way either. I was teaching new courses, on a different academic level, to students who were different from those I normally teach, and in a culture that was entirely new to me.

To convey the richness of the teaching and learning experiences in Grouard, I have decided to describe my personal encounters with several individual (yet composite) students. Perhaps, when all the pieces of the mosaic are joined together, these vignettes will illustrate my teaching techniques and problems, my failures and successes, and my feelings about living and teaching in this small northern corner of the world.

Setting The Stage

Grouard is a small town in Alberta's Peace Country, about 350 kilometers north of Edmonton. It is the site of one of the province's several Vocational Centers (AVCs), which offer upgrading courses to mainly Native or rural students who have not finished high school or who need further vocational training. I was housed in a well furnished, faculty apartment in the little town of High Prairie, Alberta. High Prairie is about a half-hour drive (or 50 kilometers) west of Grouard, which is a charming, historical Native village where the elegant, immaculate AVC building is located. This educational center offers vocational courses that range from nurse's aides to carpentry, from home household aides to computer technicians. The GMCC Social Work Program had rented space in the AVC building, and our large sunny classroom looked out on a meadow, a lake, and beautiful trees.

The landscape changed from week to week. There were two glorious weeks when the fall foliage painted the landscape yellow and gold. And then, two Mondays later, after a weekend windstorm, all the trees were bare. Next came one week when the sun was a blinding red ball that stared directly at me as I drove from High Prairie to Grouard each morning. The following week, the sun rose late enough so that I drove most of the way there in the dark. Beauty came on the drive home in the form of breathtaking sunsets in flaming skies. Just a few weeks later came the snow with its own beauty and inconvenience and my anxiety about starting the car and braving the cold in the dark early mornings. I had a habit of starting out half an hour earlier than necessary each morning, in case I needed help with my battery. I had made such a fuss about punctuality that all my students would have howled with pleasurable derision if I had ever been one minute late.

At Grouard, the coordinator of the Social Work program taught social policy and a psychologist, who also instructed at AVC, taught developmental psychology. This arrangement was very different from the usual block field placements, which alternated with a course taught in a one, two, or three-week session by visiting faculty. My students were having their *first experience* as full-time adult learners. Many of them were carrying four courses plus two days of field work, which all had to be combined with heavy family obligations. They felt quite overwhelmed with the academic pressures and field work expectations.

At that time, the two-year outreach program was taught only one year at a time, and this year was the second of the two years. A high-school diploma was required for program admission, and successful completion would provide students with an associate degree in social work. Some students would continue on for another two years in order to earn a college degree, but to do so, they would have to move away from High Prairie.

The Basics

I was assigned to teach one, six-hour class in clinical practice (Methods II) on Mondays and one three-hour class in group work on Tuesdays. Although a six-hour class seems quite long, it proved to be too short to cover all the things I wanted to teach them. The three-hour group class was definitely too short. Occasionally, we had to borrow time from the Methods class to squeeze in all the things we wanted to do in the group work class. The rest of the week was my own, and much of that time was devoted to preparing for these two classes. We had four textbooks, and I would assign about one chapter a week for each course. However, I noticed that most of my students either did not have the time, the inclination, or the ability to digest these chapters. Thus I began abstracting the chapters, distributing the abstracts in class, and using them as our teaching agenda.

In addition to the didactic teaching, we put as many concepts as possible into practice through a variety of role-play exercises, which the students not only greatly enjoyed, but also learned the most from. The majority were incredibly good actors who understood the emotional subtleties that a particular role required and threw themselves into these roles with gusto. The Methods class students worked together in pairs, and each pair carried their imaginary case from crisis intake, to referral letter, to case assessment and various interventions, through to termination. Students took turns acting as both client and counsellor in all of these phases. Most (but not all) written assignments, such as referral letters or case assessments were structured around these role play exercises.

In the group class, students also worked in pairs. Their task was to plan a group of their own choosing, decide on a particular focus and potential clients, get permission to run it, advertise it, and so on from beginning to end. We had groups for battered wives, for teenagers to learn how not to drive "under the influence," for elderly residents in an old age home, for parent education, and for other groups that matched the interests or field placements of the students. Each group eventually held live sessions with the rest of the class acting as the targeted client population. These students were then invited to evaluate how effectively the group leaders had met their goals.

The Cast of Characters

There were twenty students in my class, and I would now like to introduce you to some of them.

On the first day of class, I asked all the students to write their names on a piece of paper and tell me something about themselves. This request created some puzzlement and concern. I later understood that they were afraid that I would "psychoanalyse them," which evoked a self-protective response to hide their true selves as much as possible. Even before appearing on the scene, I knew that I would be received with a measure of suspicion and mistrust. The problem of the white missionary, with good intentions, who brought "the good word" and mixed benefits to the Native population still existed.

In terms of my own reception, there was an additional problem. My coming was widely advertised in the local papers, and my "special interest in Native students" was wrongly emphasized, along with my famous heritage. To these students, I was just one more teacher, who came on the scene, made many stringent demands, including a demand for openness, and then suddenly and quickly disappeared. The only difference was that I would be staying for a whole semester, three and a half months, while other teachers disappeared after only a few weeks. Although I tried to address these various issues early, I encountered only blank faces and the denial that any of these matters were a problem. I anticipated that it would take some time to overcome these burdens and prove myself.

Ruth

I shall start with a student I have named Ruth; her profile illustrates many of strengths and conflicts of all the Native students. Ruth is heavy set and somewhat matronly beyond her age of forty, but she has a lively mobile face. Ruth introduced herself, in writing, in the following way: *"I am married for the second time and have five children ages 19, 18, 13, 4 and 18 months. I have lived in this area for approximately eight years. My residence is in the _____ Reserve."*

To my inexperienced eyes, living on the Reserve appeared to be a doubled-edged blessing. On the one hand, a student like Ruth would be surrounded by an extended family and embedded in what might be viewed as a support network. On the other hand, the network appeared to be at least as draining as it was sustaining. Several female students (especially those from the Reserve), complained that their friends and relatives kept dropping in on weekends; they could not understand that students had to do their homework. Not being hospitable would be regarded as a serious breach of conduct and create hostility among neighbours.

In Ruth's case, as in the case of many Native students, a continual stream of extended family crises occurred, which always required her attention. For example, early in the year, her father-in-law died, which involved a funeral, other rites, and several days absence from school. Some time later, her husband had a car accident, which involved a hospitalization in Edmonton, hospital visits, and class absences. I had never worked with a group of people who had so many successive personal crises, and Ruth was certainly not an extreme case. In times of crises, students were often tempted to drop out of the program and this was true of Ruth. She had started the year with great misgivings about continuing in the program, something I learned only after reading her "log."

I had asked the students to keep a log or diary that recorded how their learnings interfaced with their lives. It was to be done, I explained, to encourage self-reflection and self-awareness and to help them lead an examined, rather than an unexamined life. These logs were handed in on the first class day of each month. I was touched and surprised with the sharing that the students did in their logs, especially when compared to their verbal reticence. They became an ongoing, private correspondence I had with each student.

Ruth did quite well in her written assignments, and I was not concerned about her failing either course. But she did not participate in class unless specifically called upon; some of these "silent members" never said a single word unless I called upon them personally.

I told the students that I would like to have lunch with each of them at least once, as my way of getting personally acquainted. These lunches, their symbolic meanings, and the conversations that ensued ended up looming large in my life at Grouard. A few students took the inititiative and asked to meet with me, while other students waited to be invited. I had expected that they would approach me. I was also cautious about asking the Native students for lunch, because I wanted to dispel the notion that I was "studying" them. It was after I had lunch with a high-status member of the group—there were such distinctions within the student body—that Ruth told me in semi-hurt tones that she also wanted to have lunch with me, and we so did the next day.

Ruth talked to me about her suspicion and resentment of white people, her suffering in the Indian School, and her unwillingness to learn "white ideas" but wanting the acceptance of the people from the predominant culture. She had worked in a local "white" hospital in High Prairie as a counsellor in charge of mediation between Native and white ideas with respect to health care. She had entered the social work program because she felt she could not do her job properly without some formal social work training. The hospital was eager to hire her back, but she was hesitant about returning to a job that depended on her being a Native person. In a white setting, she wanted to be recognized for her skills. Ruth also talked about her ambitions for her children, and how she hoped that they would all receive an education. Native people were coming into their own, and they needed the leadership of young people who had acquired skills and education.

Although friendly and open, our interchange at lunch did not improve Ruth's class participation. Instead, another event, which occurred a few weeks later, had much more significance. As part of our group work learning, I instituted a weekly student group, which ran about 30 to 60 minutes a session. After much debate, the students named it the Study Support Group. "Student Association Debates" had been a strong contender for a name, because of its acronym SAD. As the weeks passed, this student group became more and more eventful. In early November, Marilyn raised the issue of the "silent members." She did it caringly, expressing concern and interest and the wish to hear from some of the students who never voiced their opinions. I encouraged her to name these members, and Ruth was one of the students (all of whom were Native) who was identified. Ruth got very angry; she almost screamed that she was tired of being labelled a silent member in every class, and that from now on she would purposely never say anything. After the group had ended, I approached Ruth informally and told her that the chip, or rather the whole trunk, she was carrying on her shoulder was going to make it difficult for her to become a good social worker. She responded that she had grown up with feelings of suspicion and resentment and could not suddenly be rid of them.

Some weeks later, Ruth announced in the Student Support Group that she had been terribly upset because I told her she would never be a good social worker. Then she added that she had thought about her former response and apologized for the outburst, which she now saw was unjustified. She mentioned that she wanted to change and to become a more active participant. When Ruth discussed this same resolution in her diary, she wrote:

"When Marilyn mentioned about the silent member, I felt like I was being picked on and really got defensive. Later I thought a lot about what had happened and came to the conclusion that I should open up and contribute more and also learn to trust others. I will not learn anything if I do not participate. I apologized to the group for my outburst last week and believe they were concerned. I know I have to learn to

overcome my fear and silence and I still have a long way to go and I am trying and I think that's a start."

Here are some further reflections about the student support group Ruth shared with me through her log.

"Today in group we talked about the process of termination. It is sad to know we are already terminating and we have not really started. I somehow feel I missed something along the way. If I had made more effort to participate I would have got more from the group."

About three weeks before the end of the semester, Ruth began contributing to class discussions and became a more lively spontaneous participant in other activities such as role playing. I made several comments, privately and publicly, about my delight at meeting this "new Ruth," and we laughed and joked together. She appeared to be very pleased with her changing role.

Mark

Mark had had considerable professional experience according to his get-acquainted sheet, and he seems to have been a class leader. Mark, a caucasian probably in his late thirties, was a heavy set man with a paunch that bulged over his belt. He would stride through the Center, in his cowboy hat and boots, calling out greetings to various guys. He was eager to have lunch with me and to relate on a semicollegial basis and to talk about his ambition for further education. Mark made no secret of the fact that he had been through an alcohol rehabilitation program, and that this program had become his major area of professional interest, which was reflected in his current field placement and his part-time job as an alcohol counsellor. He was one of several students who had overcome problems with alcohol. Most of these students had grown up with alcohol abuse problems in their families. Mark knows his way about, he is a man of the world, and his supervisor gives him considerable responsibility. However, Mark began the year with serious health problems, which caused him to miss several classes and get behind in his school work. His son had recently shot off a gun too close to Mark's left ear, and he was now temporarily deaf in that ear and could not hear well. Mark had a chronic cold, his TB test was positive, which made him fretful, and he appeared distraught. He used one of the early student group sessions to get a handle on his weight problem, and most of the group time that day was devoted to giving Mark advice. To my surprise, he wrote in his log that he felt he had not been completely supported by the group. Nevertheless, Mark went on a strict diet and announced only two weeks later that he had lost 27 pounds and 4 ounces. He got many positive strokes from all of us for this remarkable achievement.

Mark often related to class discussions of psychological concepts. When I talked about children who felt worthless and who engaged in self-defeating behavior because they had been treated badly by their parents, he wondered if his annual February crisis, which jeopardized his career plans, was a throwback to his father literally tossing him out of the house the February he turned 16. He also related to the concept of Projective Identification, thinking his son's defiance might be an acting out of Mark's never voiced resentment of his mother. Mark's early acceptance of these psychodynamic concepts was important because initially, the class rejected or ridiculed them. However, this attitude quickly passed; it was followed by considerable fascination with, and many questions about, these concepts. It was sad that Mark's insights did not help to prevent a series of either careless or accidental mishaps, which ultimately defeated his goal of becoming a star student.

Jessica

Jessica was equally adept at bringing psychological concepts to life. When the students were asked to invent a problem to bring to a crisis counsellor, three-quarters of them role-played a wife who was being battered by an alcoholic husband whom she wanted to leave. Subsequently, each student had to write up their first interviews and assessments on this case. Their assessment papers were a monotonous repetition of similar incidents having to do with alcoholism and wife beating. The students made little attempt to individualize these situations. They did not see the problem as one that was acted out by individuals each with unique histories and various complex motivations. That day I made a semi-philosophical speech about when a problem begins, carrying it from an immediate triggering incident all the way back to prior generations. I encouraged the students to broaden their perspectives.

I illustrated my ideas using their case examples. A young woman, with a small child, lives in her mother's house on the reserve and is asking for help in dealing with her alcoholism. The woman's mother has been taking care of the young child. I examined the relationship between these two women and suggested the possibility that they may be competing for the child. I questioned how the young woman's sobriety and her subsequent ability and desire to take charge of the mothering might cause a crisis in the current mother-daughter relationship.

Jessica helped us a great deal with this problem. She volunteered the information that she had been a battered wife and that it had taken her a long time to leave her husband. Because Jessica was a vigorous, assertive, and colorful Native woman, it was difficult to stereotype her or to picture her as a typical battered wife. She was also ready to answer our questions about the dynamics (as she understood them) that led to her staying in an abusive relationship. She had been raised in a strict Roman Catholic household and divorce was forbidden. Her parents had been opposed to her early marriage, and because she had stubbornly insisted on having her own way, she was now expected to bear the consequences. Jessica's mother had also been physically abused by her father, and so the whole experience was a familiar one. She also had a son, was frightened, and was not sure how she would manage alone in the world.

Jessica was tall and slim. She and I were the only class members who wore dresses, except hers were more elegant. She enjoyed wearing colorful Native jewellery in her long black hair, along with matching earrings. Although some students secretly called Jessica an "apple" (red on the outside and white on the inside), Jessica was a strong spokesperson for Native issues and assumed the role of watchdog against class racial discrimination. For example, one student role-played a case where a young woman wanted help because she was constantly losing her temper with her young children. The woman was addicted to Bingo, and her husband was addicted to drugs. The family had some equilibrium, until the husband lost his job and there was no money for Bingo. The woman became so irritable that she began to lose her temper with her children and became really scared when she threw her three-year-old boy against the wall.

The class talked about "the problem" in this case. Was it the Bingo, the drugs, the marriage, or something else? I cautiously expressed the view that this young woman needed to develop herself as a person. Then Jessica spoke up. She made a strong statement about my imposing my middle-class values on this mother who was leading an ordinary simple life. Her strong ideas and opinions were often an energizing force in a class where lethargy and passivity were constant dangers. Jessica was a respected class leader, and I came to anticipate and appreciate her provocative questions and opinions.

I don't really know why there was a tension between Jessica and me. Fortunately it later disappeared. Perhaps it stemmed from an early confrontation in which I had commented irritably on her lateness. Jessica then asked to speak to me privately. She explained that she did the best she could, that inevitable circumstances sometimes arose, that she felt infantilized when I made a fuss about her being late, and that she wanted me to know her feelings. I expressed my feelings as well, and we made a peace of sorts. Initially, she had all her papers typed, including her diary. Hers were the only typed papers; most of the other students did not own typewriters. As our relationship thawed, Jessica began to handwrite her papers like everyone else.

Jessica looked up words in her dictionary while I taught, and asked why I sometimes used hard words. I think she was sincerely curious about my motives and asked questions, which were no doubt clarifying for herself as well as for everyone else. We had a classroom contract wherein students could ask me to clarify any words I used that were not clear to them. I explained that extending one's vocabulary was part of a professional education, and the students obviously enjoyed this game of learning new words. Favorite new words such as euphemism, narcissism, Achilles heel, and Pyrrhic victory would then appear in their next assignments.

Jessica decided to give me a personal parting gift. She asked me for private time, and I cringed at the thought that I had once again trespassed. But she only wanted to consult me about a job conflict. As we sat down together she said, "I would never have foreseen that I would want to talk to you about this difficulty!"

Peter

Peter was a slight Caucasian man, perhaps in his mid-thirties, with a rough voice and a stiff demeanor. His prior jobs included working in saw mills and logging camps. Peter was well read in politics, with a Marxist orientation that often clashed with his rigid, conservative and moralistic values. He could easily have become the group scapegoat, as he occasionally voiced outrageous ideas, but it was obvious that he was a spokesperson for some of the "non-social work attitudes" of the group. While he irritated everyone with his pronouncements, the students recognized themselves in him and forgave him. Actually the students tended to protect him and often saved him from getting into too much trouble.

For example, I suggested that abortion was one solution to a teenager's unwanted pregnancy. This solution was clearly unacceptable to most of the students, many of whom had been raised as Roman Catholics and were not used to taking that much control over their lives. Moreover, having a child, in or out of wedlock, was considered a natural and welcome part of life. The concept of illegitimacy seemed to be almost non-existent in this northern culture. Many people here lived or had lived in common-law relationships, and the rigid distinctions between marriage and non-marriage were not of much interest to them. Thus, my suggestion was met with disapproving gasps, but surprisingly, Peter's argument against abortion was also unwelcome. He felt that the girl had made a mistake and therefore, had to bear the consequences. There was some laughing objections to the thought that having a child was a punishment, and then the class became restless. There were some quick and urgent demands for a break.

A similar incident occurred when I tried to persuade the students that raising the matter of racial differences between social workers and their clients was important to a counselling situation. Several students protested vigorously; they argued that it did not really matter if a person was Native or not. Peter declared that the whole thing was far-fetched and that in a town like McLellan, for example, there was no difference because all the Natives had become like Whites. I asked him if all the Whites had also become like Natives. Peter stopped in the middle of his tirade and looked at me with confusion. He made some remark like, "I see what you mean." The class laughter was once again followed by an urgent demand for a break. I respected Peter for being willing to take risks, to challenge me, and to speak his mind. I could also sense that Peter's inner world was being transformed, perhaps to a greater degree than that of any other student.

Peter not only challenged theoretical issues, but he was also the most eloquent opponent of administrative authority. I tackled two problems early in my tenure at Grouard; first was the issue of punctuality, namely my very strict expectations for it, and second was the issue of attendance. Both issues seemed perfectly designed to allow the students to express their ambivalence to my appearance on the scene. In various contexts, they frequently alluded to my "excessive need" for punctuality. Edith sympathetically asked if I had grown up in a very rigid family that lived by the clock. Other students nostalgically recalled a former teacher who had sat on the "smoking steps" with them during breaktime and continued the class discussions. These breaks became an extension of classroom time, and "the need to return promptly after ten minutes" disappeared. Such reminiscences made me feel like a very "un-stepsitting" person. I preferred to think that my absolutely predictable time boundaries provided a safe structure for students whose lives were frequently chaotic.

The class breaks actually became an object of controversy. We started with one, 20-minute mid-morning break. When I noticed that students had a habit of leaving the classroom at odd times for unknown errands, I substituted the original break with two, 10-minute breaks. I announced that bodily needs would have to be accommodated during the break time, thus preparing them for professional practice. I then felt like a lion tamer who feared that either lethargy, chaos, or rebellion would break out if I so much as turned my back on them for more than a minute. I came to class with a lesson plan for the entire six hours, and that plan left absolutely no room for uncertain fumblings on my part.

The issue of attendance was more complicated. First of all, my request that students personally meet with me after an absence was met with great indignation and talk of being "infantilized." I responded that I could not force them to do so, but I had stated my preference. Second, the administrative guidelines allowed for three unexcused absences, but there was some uncertainty as to whether this number translated into six absences for a "double class" of six hours. I argued that out of fourteen class days (for the Methods course), three absent days should be the maximum, but this proposition was also met with vehement protest. Peter then declared that the Edmonton students did not even have "double classes" and that having a six-hour class must mean that the outreach students were inferior to the Edmonton students, and perhaps it was even illegal to expect more from one group than from the other. The idea of whether or not people considered them to be inferior to the Edmonton students touched everyone in the quick. I was convinced that I needed the full six hours to teach this group of students the expected curriculum, and the possibility of a "social action" against the six-hour class made me quite anxious. The matter resolved itself when neither the students nor I pursued this particular battle. Peter was the only one who seemed to have taken this issue seriously. In his last "letter" to me (He refused to write a log, but rather submitted occasional letters, and I did not challenge him on this preference.), he wrote:

"Our time together is coming rapidly to an end and whether this is fortunate or unfortunate remains to be seen in the future. I feel that you are starting to acculture yourself with vastly different institutions. Several complaints have been voiced pertaining to the overabundance of hours for both methods and group. As I look back, I felt and believe that I have acquired a great deal of knowledge. Sometimes have been monotonous for both of us, however I would think the majority of time has been well spent. As I look back at my time in both of your classes, I have gone from being disgruntled to being very very comfortable. I wish you luck in your travels."

It was Peter who was willing to fill me in, during our last few class sessions, on how these feelings had all started. "I was frightened to death of you and could hardly get myself to come to class," he said. He needed three classes before he could begin to relax. Other students had similar feelings of awe, which were mixed with their determination not to let me "lord it over them." Christine thought it was a joke when they announced that Freud's granddaughter was going to be their teacher. They felt relieved, surprised, and disappointed (depending on the student), that I never even talked about my grandfather. After Peter gave me his feedback on how he had gotten used to me and my ways of teaching, how he even began to appreciate them, and how he had never met anyone who even resembled me, Peter announced that he did not like goodbyes and did not attend our last class.

Celia

Peter was not the only student who voiced vigorous objections to the idea of discussing racial differences in an interview. Celia, who did not believe in *any* professional techniques, was even more adamant. She wrote in her log

I would never ask a Native person if they were uncomfortable because I was white. People here are smart and quick enough to realize if they are dealing with a worker who is uncaring or not understanding. I once asked a Native fellow who has had a tough life on the street if he felt he could talk freely to a counsellor who had not had the difficult experiences with alcohol problems he is going through. He said, "I would look into their eyes and see their heart. That's what counts."

Celia was a divorced Caucasian woman in her mid-forties with adult, problematic children. She was very soft-spoken, and my initial assessment of her face and her low lifeless voice led me to a diagnosis of chronic depression. However, as I came to know her better, I felt less sure about this diagnosis. Celia's log indicated an extremely caring and generous person. She allowed street people and alcoholics to stay overnight at her home even though she was living on the verge of poverty herself. She supported herself by waitressing in High Prairie. I believe the idea of becoming a professional person, and perhaps distancing herself by that definition from other poor and deprived people, was morally repugnant to her.

Peter, Celia, and a number of other students had trouble coming to terms with the idea that one did not have to answer every question that a client asked. Celia thought that was positively unethical and unfair. Not only, these students insisted, were counsellors expected to share their similar problems, but also to describe what they had done about them. For instance, if the counsellor had also been a battered wife who left her husband, then she should say so, but she should add that her situation and every case was different. We had heated class discussions about this issue. I set up a role play in which Celia played a client who was expecting an unplanned child and was uncertain what to do about it. I was the social worker and Celia was to ask me about my experience with this situation. Celia did as instructed, and I answered (with a hint of superiority in my voice) that all my children had been planned for the very month in which they had been born. There was much uproar in the class, and I believe I convinced most students that truthful, self-disclosing answers were not necessarily beneficial for the client.

Celia was a good student, and she wrote fine papers and quizzes. But the very idea of a "professional interview" terrified her. She also worked in a setting where she did not handle personal clients, and I believe she was relieved about that. Celia was not sure if she could be a social worker. I suggested that she would make an excellent advocate and advised she seek a position that required such skills. She said she would think about this.

Monique

Monique was the intellectual star of the class. Although she vocally objected to my attendance demands, she would not have dreamed of missing a single class. She attended class for weeks with walking pneumonia, which I finally diagnosed for her, and went to a doctor only after I insisted. She disagreed with most of the ideas I brought up in the first few weeks and told me that she was known to be a disagreeing person. Then, her thirst for knowledge and deeper understanding became more important than her need to maintain her rebellious persona. Interestingly, her log indicated that she began insisting on punctuality and attendance in the single-parent group she was co-leading in her field placement. Almost imperceptibly she switched from the role of the rebel to the role of teacher's assistant. Whenever I could not find the right words or the correct illustration to clarify a particular concept, I would turn to Monique, who always found the magic explanation for her student colleagues.

I developed a profound admiration for Monique's intellect. She was a tall, strong-looking woman, who dressed in rough clothes. During our first lunch meeting, she told me that she was married to a Native man whom she loved deeply. He had been unemployed for six months, which had been hard on them and their family of four young children, and they were currently living in a trailer. Recently, her husband had gotten a job clearing brush for an oil exploration firm. Monique and I met twice more over lunch, and I spent most of my time telling her what a wonderful mind she had and begging her to develop her intellectual potential. But Monique, like Celia, was worried about becoming co-opted by education. In my feedback to her log entries, I expressed the hope that she might eventually find a compromise between "being professional and being a real person."

Monique was also clearly uncomfortable about asking potentially indiscreet and/or intrusive questions. Such standard social work techniques were especially distasteful to the culture of the Native students, who felt these inquiries were contrary to respectful social intercourse. I tried to persuade them that asking questions could also be regarded as a sign of interest and caring, but I don't think I convinced them.

Monique decided to take a risk during our student support group session. She explained that she had read something about domineering personalities and it seemed to be an apt description of herself. She wanted to know how the other students saw her. No other student would ever have taken that kind of risk, although some mentioned in their logs that they wished they had the courage to do so. Florence, who was the silent yet incontrovertible leader in the class, spoke up. She told Monique that she was "all head and no heart," and because heart was more important to Florence than head, she could not respect Monique. They discussed some episode in which a misunderstanding had occurred between these two powerful women. Monique started to cry. Other students began to take sides. Marilyn said that Monique had such a domineering way of voicing her opinions that she left no room for any other views. Peter got up and said that he would not be witness to this kind of unfair persecution, and to everyone's consternation, he left the classroom. The session continued, and Monique got various kinds of feedback; some was unkind and perhaps motivated by jealousy, some was very positive and admiring. The tensions that existed between Florence and Monique, which were apparently well known to the class and certainly to both women, were openly discussed for the first time. During break the two women got together and made peace.

Monique would later write in her log that it had been an exhilarating occasion for her, tears and all. When we reassembled after this dramatic group event, the whole class, Monique included, challenged Peter's brusque departure. Peter conceded that he might have been more effective staying with the group and voicing his opinion. The incident was a high point in our student support group, which I felt had previously lacked a spirit of vigor and risk-taking. Monique's parting log was deeply precious to me:

Thank you again for our talks. You have given me much to think about plus a booster shot. I was thinking that one of my most important learnings this year was that of owning your own feelings. ... I was amazed at the amount of power this releases in you. Once you admit them then you can begin work on what to do with them. I feel as if we are getting to know each other and that our time has run out too fast. I appreciate the time you have given us and I wish you good luck and God blessings on your journey.

Sonja

The other student who left at midday on the last day of class was Sonja. She was angry with me because I had given her some critical feedback on her last paper. She had written up her "best case" about a welfare client who had stolen from the state, and then "given her a very hard time." I should not have imposed unrealistic standards on Sonja with respect to getting to know her client and showing some curiosity about the client's way of living. Her client was a Native woman who had a habit of spending every penny she received from any source as fast as possible on various luxury items. After the money was gone, she would throw herself on the mercy of the social assistance department, who could not let her and her children starve, or freeze to death, or get thrown out of the flat due to non-payment of rent. Sonja thought the woman "did not know how to manage money;" my view was that she had found quite an effective way of managing the system.

Although Sonja got an A in both of her courses, I was sorry that I was critical. I simply did not have the heart to give her less than the best grade, given her conscientiousness, her hard work, and her deep concern about doing a perfect job. She was a woman who liked rules, liked to follow them exactly, got upset when they were broken. She also became disoriented and angry when unexpected things happened or when directions were unclear, such as what she was supposed to write in her log. The inevitable arbitrary nature of grades led to a series of tense interactions between us. We had several quizzes in each of our courses, and Sonja argued angrily about each point that I took off from her answers. I always dreaded reviewing her quizzes and added extra points, just to avoid these tedious arguments. In fairness to Sonja, I must add that arguing about grades was unfortunately endemic among my students.

Sonja lived on a reserve. She felt some bitterness about the fact that the Band was not financing her education because she was only living "common-law" with her Native husband. She felt much conflict about being in school. She felt torn between attending to the health needs of her baby, struggling with her husband's opposition to her going to school, and her own desire to finish the program and become a social assistance worker, a position for which I considered her well suited.

Edith

Many of the married female students felt unsupported by husbands who were either inconvenienced by their wives' heavy academic schedules or threatened by being surpassed educationally. A nearby literacy program for Mennonite women had had to close because the husbands had forced their wives to discontinue learning. The matter was of special concern to Edith.

Edith was one of the women who was close to my age and one of the few students who had welcomed me with an appreciative and open spirit. She and her husband, a part-time truck driver, lived on a farm and had raised 11 children, several of whom were special needs children they had adopted. Edith was worried about whether or not her husband would like "her new self" and indeed, their marriage deteriorated over the months that I knew her. Her kindness and good judgement enabled her to interview with ease. I often chose her to be "the worker" when demonstrating difficult situations such as investigating child neglect complaints.

Edith had invited me to have dinner with their family, but I felt I had to decline. While I would have enjoyed meeting all my students in their family settings, I did not want to be accused of favoritism.

When the issue of homosexuality was raised in the course of our class discussions, I took the opportunity to do some strong educational advocacy. After class, Edith consulted me about her son who came home to "come out" to his parents. He was extremely anxious and full of self-doubts. I arranged two, very private, low-key appointments with her son and had the deeply gratifying experience of seeing a small intervention make a considerable difference to a young man and his family.

Marilyn

Marilyn was also worried about my being lonely, and in spite of my reassurances, she repeatedly invited me to attend the local ice hockey games "with the crowd." Yet I felt she was one of the students who carefully kept me at arm's length. I call her Marilyn because she looked like Marilyn Monroe and could easily have been a model. She was another single mother who supported herself and her child while attending school. Marilyn also had her "three allowable absences," and when I questioned her about her attendance, she replied with a piqued expression that "it has not been more than three times for each course." She repeatedly handed in her assignments late, and while I was initially rather lax about this matter, I eventually became irritated. I felt that the students were taking advantage of my not having a policy whereby each late assignment would be graded down. I told the class that my respect for them as adults was related to their honoring their commitments. When Marilyn handed in her third paper late, without any explanations, I made an angry comment which she accepted with a hurt expression. Although these events cooled our relationship, Marilyn's work was invariably of high quality. She had a quick mind and completed the quizzes in about half the time that other students needed, often 80% or 90% correctly.

Our first dramatic encounter occurred when Marilyn remained unpaired for an exercise she needed to complete for her homework. It was my habit to pair with students on such occasions, and I told her that we would be working together. She would have to interview me and write an assessment of our initial interview. Marilyn was aghast. She pleaded and begged not to be my partner. She explained that "Methods" was her weak area and that she was not ready to interview me. After some rapid soul searching, I insisted that we work together. At the time, I was working with a client who had been molested by her father, and I decided to impersonate her. Marilyn proved to be caring and helpful throughout the interview, which gave both of us enormous pleasure and relief.

Later, I read in Marilyn's log that she felt that she was once again defeating her own purpose by her late papers. She wished I would give her some kind of feedback because she felt everyone was needlessly "picking on her." I invited her to lunch on the second last day of classes. I understood how much that invitation meant to her when another student asked me if I was free for lunch that day. When Marilyn overheard this request she said, "She is lunching with me," and stuck out her tongue in triumph! Thinking back, I believe I did not need to be quite so cautious about intruding upon my students' lunchtimes.

My own preoccupation with maintaining law and order in the classroom blinded me to Marilyn's rather desperate hunger for approval. I explained to her how she had alienated me, and she reported that her supervisor had given her similar feedback. She felt she wanted to do something about her manner and her life. She entered counselling after finding out that AVC students were entitled to free counselling services. (She was one of two students who had decided to go into counselling at the end of that term.) I also used this opportunity to give Marilyn credit for her high academic performance and applauded her plans to continue her education in a big city.

Anise and Trudi

There were two Native women in the class whom I could not reach. Anise had big brown eyes and a permanent uncertain smile on her face. As a student, was a silent, uncertain, and lost woman who was unprepared to meet the demands of the material, either orally or in writing. However, there was an aura of sensitivity and gentleness about her, which was extremely appealing. I am sure that she must have functioned differently in other settings. Although she had a social service position on the Reserve, she gave me no evidence of this other, different self. Her greatest difficulty stemmed from the fact that the Band might not continue to pay her tuition if she failed and she might never have another chance to receive formal training. Unfortunately, my responsibilities as a teacher interfered with my more humanistic concerns. I could not give Anise a passing grade.

Although Trudi was also a Native woman, she was older, sturdier, and at times, quite fiercely self-assertive. Although she had more than sufficient ability to do the work and considerable psychological sophistication, she put up a wall against oral and written assignments and closed her mind to any possibility of learning. Here is the letter that I wrote to Trudi:

December 18, 1987

Dear Trudi:

I had to fail you in Methods and give you a D in groupwork. I want to tell you exactly how I feel about this, even though you will no doubt think that I am hypocritical and just saying all these things. I really care about you and respect you and I wish we could have gotten closer, but initially you avoided me out of lack of trust and toward the end when we might have gotten closer, I started to feel so badly about your poor performance and you felt equally badly, so I could no longer reach out to you, although I made small tries.

Your writing is actually quite fluent and you can express yourself clearly in both writing and speaking when you are in the mood and I don't understand why the material is quite so difficult for you because you have a perfectly good head. I feel as if there is an emotional obstacle that you have erected against learning and that the problem is in your feelings rather than in your mind because I have the impression that you are very smart. I believe that you are so two-sided about completing or not completing the program that you are only half present (and often you are absent without ever giving me an explanation). Perhaps having always one foot in and one foot out takes away your energy from learning. I went over all the material in class, so that even if you had not read it, and just listened carefully in class, you could have learned it that way. You did not choose to participate in the student support group, even though you have had much group experience and could have helped the group along. I don't know why you don't want to give more of yourself in the classroom situation. As a social worker you have to learn to be generous to others, rather than withholding. I have already said goodbye to you on your log and now I say it again. I loved my teaching experience up here but I feel frustrated and defeated by our encounter. I would have liked to help you in your goal of becoming a good social worker and I think I could have done so if you had let me. I hope you can repeat the course and do well next time around. I wish you very well for your future.

Sophie

Trudi then wrote me a letter. In it she explained that I had reminded her of someone with whom she had had a very difficult relationship and that was the reason she could not learn with me. I do not question this explanation, but I wish she could have talked to me about these strong feelings. Trudi also had difficulty in other classes, so perhaps this reason was not the whole story. I would attribute her story and many others to the legacy of the difficult historical and socio-cultural conditions of the Native Canadian tribes.

Michael

Michael was 22 years old, a slim young man, and as I would learn, a sportsman. In class, the students sat in a square, U-shape arrangement and always in the same places. Michael and Marilyn sat opposite me, often whispering, making jokes, exchanging notes, and generally making me feel self-conscious. Michael wrote on his introductory note, *"I have poor speling,"* (sic) and no more. At the end of the semester, I reminded him of our dubious beginnings, and he said he had just meant that note as a funny joke. When I did not buy his explanation, he admitted that he had wanted it understood that he didn't want to be psychoanalysed by me. I had gotten the message and tiptoed around him for a long time.

After Michael had presented his first role play in "the Bingo-addiction" case, my respect for him grew and I recognized his talents. When I gave him my feedback to that effect as well as my reactions to his private jokes, he completely stopped the fooling around activities. During our lunch together I asked him if he took himself seriously. He told me about his ambitions and his success in sports and about how much he cared for the children in the Youth Detention Center, which was his second-year placement. Michael was cautious in the student support group, and in class, he tended to speak up only when he was directly addressed. He had a habit, either through a shrug or a grimace, of disqualifying himself whenever he made a statement, and he seemed pleased rather than offended when I pointed this mannerism out to him.

Michael was willing to learn. He won my unmitigated admiration with his last paper in which he described the work he had done with a delinquent, 15-year-old Native boy in the detention center. I persuaded Michael to allow me to read the piece in class and to send a copy of his paper to Edmonton as a sample of what our students were achieving. At first he was very dubious; he wondered if the boy would like him to do that. I reminded him that the boy might want other kids to know they could be helped the way he was helped. Not only had Michael done a magnificent piece of therapeutic work, he had also used all the concepts in our course to analyze his activities. It was the biggest gift a student could give a teacher.

The Final Curtain

I had been fretting for weeks about how I would get my four heavy suitcases from my second-floor apartment to the car, and somehow Michael's paper enabled me to ask him for help. He accepted without hesitation. Perhaps, I too can learn that it is alright to ask people for help.

I was leaving early the next morning, and I had said goodbye to all of my students at the end of our afternoon class. There had been many last minute requests for private luncheons, most of which had to be turned down. I had come into my students lives, won their confidence, and was now betraying them by going away.

That evening, Michael carried my heavy suitcases to the car and assured me that they were slightly lighter than the calves on the farm. I spent my last evening in High Prairie making friends with Michael. Although it was a happy thing to do, it just meant saying goodbye to one more person I now cared about. Michael told me how his grandparents had rescued him when he was 12 years old. Michael remembered how he had been a "bad boy" for several years, testing this new family. But his grandfather had withstood every test and eventually became his deeply loved new father. Michael considered himself very fortunate. "I wish you could meet my grandfather," he said to me, "I think you would really like each other." When I served him tea in a cup and saucer, Michael decided I was just as fussy as his grandmother and actually looked a bit like her. Suddenly, on my last evening in High Prairie I had the wonderful luck of seeing the Northern Lights.

My Canadian diary ends with the following words:

> *Today is Wednesday, Christmas Day, 1987. I left High Prairie exactly one week ago. I miss my students. I miss High Prairie. It hurts.*

References

Corey, M.S. & Corey, G. (1987). *Groups: Process and practice.* Monterey, CA: Brooks/Cole.

Hepworth, D.H. & Larsen, J. (1986). *Direct social work practice: Theory and skills.* Chicago, IL.: Dorsey Press.

Kadushin, A. (1983). *The social work interview.* New York: Columbia Unversity Press.

Shulman L. (1984). *The skills of helping.* (2nd ed.). Itasca, IL.: Peacock.

Chapter 10

Healing the Wound and the Promise of the New Sun

Pam Colorado

Prologue

There's an understanding among life forms that takes away all the hurt and loneliness a person can feel. Sometimes the communication comes in quiet, small moments; at other times ...

Introduction

The drive from the Edmonton airport to High Level, Alberta took nearly ten hours. Although I knew it would be a long haul, I welcomed the journey because it provided transition time, a way to leave my everyday life behind and to really arrive in the community of High Level. I would be teaching macro social work; this course would also be my third and final meeting with these students. Reverend Edyne Decker, a colleague and good friend, had volunteered to join me. She flew from California for the chance to visit, to experience the beauty of the North and its people, and for something else—to savor the intangible, elusive essence that somehow seemed connected to this place.

Eight hours into the drive, fatigue caught me. I began to drive faster in an attempt to outrace my sleepiness. It was near midnight. Mile after mile the black ribbon of highway flowed. Dark, pointy shadows of spruce trees whizzed by. Mesmerized, I nearly missed the orange blur that streaked through the headlights. Edyne called out, "Look, a fox!" I stopped the car and glanced back. The fox stood, framed by the roadside's dry, brown grass, and returned our stare. A black, happy smile seemed to cross his face. Rolling up the window, I happened to look up. High in the night sky, the Northern Lights spun, waved, and streamed pale green-blue and pink iridescence. Stunned, we both got out of the car and moved off by ourselves for a private moment of prayer.

After a few moments, we stood together and looked up in wonder. The Elders say that you can talk to the Aurora; that you can hear them "zinging" their responses. We also believe that these Lights are the shadows of the spirits dancing in another dimension. For this reason, we are always happy to see the Borealis but also very respectful.

Touching

A number of years ago, a young Native man who had recently become a Christian, ridiculed the deep-hued red Borealis. His friend warned him and begged him to make amends to the spirits. The young Christian laughed. Three days later, he was dead.

This story exemplifies the tensions that are triggered when Native and Western minds meet. In this case, both worlds collided within one Native man, who paid the ultimate price for not resolving the conflict. From the time of first contact through to the modern period, it has been Native people who have borne the burden of this stress. Now, as we enter the post-modern era, the consequences and limitations of the linear, Cartesian mind have brought us face to face with the extinction of the entire Native culture. It is not easy to decipher the twists and turns in the history of western thought that have so distorted our lives.

Western linear thought, the foundation of social work theory, perceives the universe as a mechanism whose operations can be controlled given enough information. There is no God, only laws of motion. All things can be known and understood by analyzing them and breaking them down into their most simple form such as subatomic particles (Kunosu, 1990). We humans have become God's mechanics, formulating and applying the new mechanical science (Metzner).

In social work, we teach counselling skills by dividing the client interview process into several parts. Because this approach seems logical, Western-thinking educators are not likely to see the monocultural imperialism underlying the educative process. In the High Level classroom, we were shocked to discover that some terms, which describe the stages of intervention, are the same as the military and political terms used for invading and expropriating people (eg. termination.) How can we continue to teach and model such dissonance while urging our students to be present for their clients?

This scientific blindness is not due to faulty character; it is an outcome of the modern era and, and at present, the essential challenge of postmodernism. Thomas Berry, Canada's esteemed environmentalist, believes that we must learn to converse with the other forms of life around us, to learn the language necessary for such communication. *The United Nations Report on the Environment* states that the last reservoirs for such language lie with the tribal peoples of the world. Berry suggests that understanding the Indian presence in this hemisphere will be one of the next stages in the development of an Earth-centered consciousness.

Transpersonal psychologist, Metzner (1993) suggests that it is possible for us to recall certain pre-industrial values that have been lost, and he calls for a technology directed toward the preservation and restoration of the damaged ecosystems that support all forms of life. He notes that the indigenous peoples of the world, with their so-called "primitive animistic" and "shamanistic" beliefs, have always practised the sustainable lifestyles that we are only now trying to develop. Then, Metzner makes the following connection between Native Americans and European Americans:

> The situation becomes even more hopeful and our chances of overcoming the consequences of the European... superiority complex are even better; when we realize that not only have other cultures ... not had this division (with nature) but our own pre-scientific and pre-Christian ancestors also did not have it. The religion and world view of the Celtic, Germanic, Baltic and Slavic peoples ... were animistic and shamanistic ... I do believe it is possible for Christians, Jews and Muslims to reconnect with the nature religion of their ancestors, and that when they do so a tremendous spiritual revitalization can take place, in which the natural world and the divine world are recognized as one and the same ...
>
> Metzner, 1993 (p. 9)

Social work was born of holism. Therefore, it is only appropriate that Native social work educators should try to link the two systems of knowledge. Although the Grant MacEwan Community College Social Work program is minute in comparison to the larger, global environmental and cross-cultural issues, it may be a crucible for regaining the authentic Native mind for both European and Native Americans alike.

The process, which is contained in the double hours format of the Native Social Work program, involves several steps. German psychologist and scholar, Kremer, speaks of an "archaeology of the mind" to describe the ways that may lead to the recovery of the tribal mind within Euro-centered traditions. To create a new pattern from the current epistemological chaos, Kremer calls for "remembrance" of the times before the dissociation began.

> Remembrance will reanimate the denied parts of ourselves which is essential if we are to avoid further ecological catastrophes, genocide, etc. The process of remembering is akin to dream recall or mythic stories.

It is not neat, it is messy. Part of this process is a reevaluation of what science has afforded us —what ills and what goods. Another aspect ... is grieving for what we have given up and lost. *It is not only that indigenous peoples are challenged to integrate scientific knowledge from their own cultural perspective, but that western peoples are challenged to integrate scientific knowledge from the perspective of the European tribal wind.*

Kremer, 1993

Prior to the detribalization of the Earth, all people had access to the whole or good mind. Native social work education recalls the essential split between mankind and nature and so opens the door to a new consciousness for all.

Coherence

In earlier chapters, I wrote about identity and the need for coherence in the classroom. I presented the concept of "presence" and pointed out the critical need for both the instructor and the student to be present.

- You will notice that I speak directly to you the reader. This formal address is not acceptable in Western scientific writing, but it is the *sine qua non* of indigenous knowledge. To be valid, knowledge must be experienced. Elders say, "put yourself in it!"

- I have mentioned, the rapture of the North, the minus 40 degree temperatures, spruce trees, thunder, lightning, rain, and snow owls. I did this because nature is the text to Native knowledge and these things happened exactly as I have described them.

- Time is a cross-cultural conundrum. To the Westerner, it is separate from space or material form. To the Native mind, there is no separation. This connection means that we can be at home wherever we are, that we value accommodation not control, and that we can communicate with life from both the past and future (as the linear mind conceives it). Thus, I can speak of meeting the ancestors on the owl's ground.

- Natives perceive the universe and its myriad life forms to be intelligent and related. Our life task and joy is to understand and complete these relationships. It is easy to agree that other beings have intelligence; it is quite another matter to establish communication and to fulfil the intent of those relationships. That is why I have shared my experience with the owl. However, I have omitted several elements of the owl story because the Native Mind teaches the principle of non-interference. The listeners must interpret the meaning for themselves. To tell everything of a spiritual event is the equivalent of speaking for God.

- The Native Mind recognizes many realities and different dimensions of consciousness. The way we become centered or complete with life is through the Good Mind. To get there, we embark on a journey. The travels that brought me to the North also opened up a consciousness that enables me to write with regard to the natural and spiritual world. Although some Western readers may ridicule or misunderstand this style, I write my Native mind anyway. This is my way of being present to you. It feels good and clean.

- We believe in sharing. Therefore, I have tried to share my Native knowledge, as I know it, with you, and I have tried to interpret it with regard to social work education.

- History is important because the Native mind seeks ultimate causality not immediate or direct causality.

- As much as possible, I have also described my feelings. Feelings and love are the hallmark of the Good Mind and a pathway to the Great Spirit of Life.

Summary

My friend Reverend Decker has been widowed for 14 years. Her late husband was a healer, and the two of them travelled the world together on various human and spiritual development projects. Edyne still grieves. That night, out on the Northern highway, something wonderful and mysterious happened. Unbeknownst to me, Edyne had written a book about her husband's practice, which was explained in terms of the Aurora Borealis. He had told her that if he should go before her, she could find him in the Northern Lights. She had never seen them before, but on this night during unseasonably warm weather, the sky was alive. I don't know for certain what she saw, but I do know that she experienced an enormous relief. She said:

> *You know, this reminds me of the first Indian ceremony I ever went to. It was long, gentle, and nice but I was expecting fireworks. Then, I walked out and everything changed!*

Edyne is not Native, but she experienced the healing of the Good Mind because being whole, experiencing with all of our senses, and communicating with the natural world is a normal, human ability. To be effective with Native people, instructors must be willing to become true partners with the Native people and to join their students in the transformational process of recovery. The process begins when each of us tries to answer Cyrus Peck's question, "Who are you?"

References

Ashley, H. (1993). Traditional Navajo practitioner. Personal Correspondence.

Bastien, B., Colorado, P. & Kunosu, S., et al (1990). *Indian Association of Alberta child welfare needs assessment and recommendations.* Edmonton, AB:

Berry, T. (1988). *The dream of the earth.* San Francisco, CA: Sierra Club Books.

Kremer, J. (1993). Personal Correspondence.

Metzner, R. (1993). The split between spirit and nature in western consciousness. *The Noetic Sciences Review.*

Chapter 11

A Return to the Circle

William Pelech

The Vision

Long ago, the great Dene Tha prophet Nogha (Wolverine) shared the following vision, which I believe is an appropriate introduction to this chapter:

> This earth is large, but we pray for the whole earth. When we go into the Tea Dance circle, then we pray, just like the priest offers communion. The prophets talk about the future and then come to God's land. This message is not just for this one place, but for the whole world. I hope it will help you all.

> Even though there is only one person left to dance, you will not be tired, and you will have the strength to sing for him as he dances. God made this land, and we should follow God's ways. Do not throw away your traditions. Continue to offer tobacco on the fire. In the future we may be confused, and we may not know who the prophet

will be...Whoever is the singer will sing without becoming tired, and a place of prayer will appear before him. He will be reborn, becoming a new person. Some people go to sleep and they dream. Then- hey!-they hear a song, they hear something good with their ears. They wake up and they remember, yes, they sing and it becomes a song...You must all help the singer.

(pp. 67, 73–74)

For countless generations, the People came together in the fall and the spring to give thanks to the Creator. They came to the Tea Dance where they would pray, share, feast, and dance. In the centre of the ring was a fire where the food would be cooked and the offering made. The fire symbolized the Creator, the source of all life. Later, the drummers and singers sang prayer songs and the dance would begin. The People all came into the circle and danced. They danced sunwise to the heartbeat of the drums. They danced as one, following the eternal circle of life as so many had done before them. Although Nogha spoke of those who became confused and left the circle, hope remains as long as there are those who return to the circle to dance.

Beginnings

In 1983, as a neophyte social worker having recently graduated from the University of Victoria, I was hired by the Department of Indian Affairs to work as a social worker in the High Level area of Northern Alberta. Armed with my copy of Pincus and Minahan (1973), I, a most eager "change agent," began working with the four First Nations in this district. I quickly learned that, although I had graduated from a rural, generalist school, my academic experience had done little to prepare me for entry into Indian communities. I realized that I had a great deal to learn. My most valuable resources were the community social workers employed by each of the First Nations.

In 1985 I became the Director of the Dene Tha Social Development Program. At that time, it became very clear that in order to help heal the community we first needed to heal ourselves. This healing process began with an eight-week, lifeskills course which included a culturally oriented group process facilitated by Martha ManyGrey Horses. With the recruitment of Gloria Denechoan as Director of the Dene Tha Counselling Program in 1987, we initiated a series of semi-annual intensive staff retreats. Our circle of staff healing grew from eight to twenty. Long-standing family conflicts and resentments among staff members were wiped away by sharing of our hurts, dreams, and humanity.

In 1988, the Board of Chiefs of the High Level Tribal Council responded to opportunities to develop child welfare services. They formed an Education and Training Committee whose mandate was to plan the on-site delivery of post-secondary education programs in the areas of social work, teaching, nursing, and administration. The Committee, headed by Clarence Fournier, Executive Director, and his wife Adele, Secretary, obtained funding to conduct a needs assessment to identify the important elements required in a Social Work program for the members of the four First Nations. In the fall of 1989, Grant MacEwan Community College was chosen as the institutional delivery agent, and the following summer, the Aboriginal Social Work Program began. I was appointed Coordinator of this program.

The program was designed and delivered according to a comprehensive planning process developed by the Education and Training Committee of the High Level Tribal Council. The Committee was directly involved in the development of the innovative program design and continues to monitor its progress. The program contained the following major elements:

- *Foundations.* In August, 1990, 29 students began the Foundations Program. The program included: personal development (three weeks), field experience (nine weeks), and English upgrading (eight weeks). Funding for the program's delivery was provided by Employment and Immigration Canada. Student support was provided by each First Nation's program.
- *Community-based learning.* One of the principles established by the Committee was to have as much of the program as possible based in the student's own

community. As a result, courses were delivered in two week blocks and alternated with two weeks of field placement. This enabled students, especially during the first year, to serve as they learned within their own communities.

- *Coursework.* The Committee required that the program include the normal pattern of social work courses as well as fully transferable arts electives such as sociology, anthropology, and political science. The duration of each course was generally increased by 33%. This additional time allowed for greater integration and application of the course content. It also gave students more time to discuss questions and explore ideas with instructors who were not based in the High Level area, and thus, not readily accessible.

In January, 1991, 26 students began the two-year Social Work Program. The students who entered the Program represented all of the reserves that comprise the four-member First Nations Tribal Council.

Twenty-two of these students completed the first trimester and 19 completed the second trimester. Our students differed from their urban counterparts, who attended the program in Edmonton, in the following ways:

- All were aboriginal or treaty Indians.
- All were residents of one of the reserves of the four-member First Nations.
- Most of the students had lived all of their lives in isolated northern communities.
- Most spoke and wrote English as their second language.
- Most attended this program as first-time students in post-secondary education.

Eighteen female students and one male student entered the second year of the program. They ranged in age from 21 to 57 years. This attrition rate compared favourably with other similar projects.

Program Assumptions

Because of their experiences in the North and their personal acquaintance with the students who had been admitted to the Program, the members of the Education Committee stressed the need for integrating personal development sessions into the program. They based this request on the following assumptions:

- The Social Work Program itself is a personal development process, and many students had experienced unresolved personal issues which could be triggered by course materials and field placement experiences. For example, all students would have had direct or indirect experiences with residential schools.

- Although many students had experienced substantial losses, they may not have had access to personal development and recovery programs in their own communities.

- All students must have an opportunity to access a therapy process to resolve their personal issues so that they, in turn, could be empowered to help other community members deal with similar issues.

- The program could reinforce the students' personal and cultural strengths by integrating Native cultural and spiritual practices into the personal development process.

Program Design

The personal development process was integrated into the program design in the following ways:

- *Counselling.* Both the instructors and I provided counselling services to students on an individual basis throughout the course of the program.

- *Support groups.* We regarded the student body as a community. To promote linkages between the students, five family groups were formed of four to six students each. These groups, which were selected and named by the students, included the Ray of Hope, Doves, Eagles,

Thunderbirds, and Sunshine families. Regular family group meetings were held with me to discuss individual issues as they emerged.

- *Personal development weeks.* During each trimester, students had an opportunity to participate as clients in an intensive group experience. A total of seven group sessions were held over a 29-month period. Each session lasted five days. These sessions were designed to help students explore personal issues triggered during class or field placements. The first six sessions were held in the classroom and the final session at a residential retreat. Attendance was voluntary and each student participated to the extent that he or she felt comfortable.

The Journey – The Classroom Experience

One of the program's main thrusts was the empowerment of each student's sense of self and the reinforcement of his or her cultural identity. This process was supported through special course development initiatives and by the instructional staff.

Consistent with the spirit of the community college movement, considerable effort was placed on the redesign and development of courses that met the needs of the First Nations and their students. This process did not entail the dilution or deletion of core course concepts, but rather the enhancement of existing course materials and the application of course concepts to the students' communities and lives. For example, a new anthropology course was created, which focused on contemporary Native issues. It was oriented to Native students learning about themselves rather than non-Native students learning about Natives. Similar changes were made to other courses including Family Dynamics, Family Violence (Methods IV), and two political science courses. A selected issues course was adapted to focus on addictions (delivered by the Nechi Institute) and suicide.

A special effort was made to recruit Native instructors and instructors who had previous experience teaching Native students. Field trips and guest speakers from local reserves were incorporated into the students' educational experience.

These initiatives culminated in the Advanced Micro-Practice (Methods II) and Community Practice (Methods III) courses. We were honoured to have Dr. Kim Zapf and Dr. Pam Colorado from the University of Calgary as instructors for Methods II. The most powerful aspect of this course involved a comparison between Western and traditional Native helping processes. Dr. Zapf presented the conventional, five-phase Western model of engagement, assessment, contracting, implementation, and termination. Dr. Colorado presented the traditional holistic and transpersonal Native model of helping.

All students found this course to be both challenging and difficult. Our more traditional Native students related well to the traditional helping model; they found the Western model's analytical and linear form to be alien and unworkable within their communities. Our less traditional Native students felt the Western model was more familiar; for them, the traditional helping model was difficult to grasp. Some of these students felt that they "got nothing out of this course" in terms of learning new counselling skills. We later discovered what this anger and resistance was really all about.

Throughout this debate, I found myself growing more and more uncomfortable with the Western model. Finally, I realized why. The terms used in this model reflect the invasion process that traditionally governed colonial relationships between Natives and Europeans. The term engagement could refer to the initial contact phase where some degree of equality and interdependence existed between the two. Assessment reflects the European colonizers' identification of the strengths and vulnerabilities (i.e. military, political, techno-logical) of the Native communities with a view toward their cultural or physical genocide. Contracting was the vehicle they used to achieve this hidden agenda, while at the same time promising a better life for Native people. In physical terms, implementation meant murder, forced starvation, or the spread of infectious disease; in cultural terms it meant the imposition of the residential school system. Of course, termination speaks for itself as the "final solution" sought by the colonial invaders. Over the past ten years, I have witnessed the consequences and devastation brought about by this invasion, and it was this same invasive nature of the Western model that I found so disturbing. Further, this awareness has caused me to question the appropriateness of teaching the Western model to Native students or to anyone else who intends to practice social work in Native communities.

The proverbial "other shoe" finally dropped during the Community Practice (Methods III) course, also instructed by Dr. Colorado. In the summer of 1992, several students approached me prior to the start of classes. They were concerned that they would be similarly disappointed with Dr. Colorado's course. One student indicated that she would not participate in the course, even if it meant that she would not graduate. I encouraged these students to share their concerns with Dr. Colorado. During our regular morning circles, these students remained seated in their chairs and refused to participate in the traditional ceremony. This situation continued for several days. Dr. Colorado finally confronted the students about their disrespect for the circle and the process. Later, when one of these students was challenged to explore her culture, she responded, "What culture?" At last, the students came to realize what their anger was really about. They were experiencing the underlying feelings of loss associated with their identities as Native people. It was at this point that they took their first step toward rediscovering their culture and themselves. One of these students later volunteered to prepare the altar each morning for our sweet grass ceremony.

Personal Development Sessions

Paralleling the in-class work, were the five-day personal development sessions. One or more of these sessions was offered during each semester of the program. The program contained seven personal development sessions.

Session One: Returning to the Circle

During the Foundations Program the students were introduced to the personal development process. This first session included trust and relationship-building exercises.

The students were supported in sharing their personal feelings and thoughts in small, and later, in large group sessions. During these five days, the family support groups were organized and morning rituals were developed. The students wanted to start each morning with a large group circle and prayer, which was followed by a brief small group "where are we?" or "check-in" session.

Session Two: Finding a Balance

During the second session, which was delivered one day a week during the Foundations Program, specific issues were explored. They included study skills, financial management, community resources and counselling services, developmental needs and experiences, and relaxation techniques.

Session Three: Facing the Fear

At this session, held the third week in December, the students were asked to explore their childhood experiences through the use of drawings and other exercises. These activities helped students to deal with physical and sexual abuse issues, the loss of parents, separation issues resulting from being sent to residential schools, the death of children and other family members, and spousal assault. By the end of this week, students had developed their own self-care programs.

Session Four: The First Steps

The fourth session was held about four months later at the end of the winter trimester. By this time, students were able to explore their personal issues further, and a second therapist was hired to work with the group. Large group relaxation and self-awareness exercises (e.g., death meditation) helped students to touch on these issues again. Small therapy groups allowed each student an opportunity to deal with these personal issues. A variety of gestalt, family sculpturing, and reconstruction techniques were used. At the end of this week, most students had completed some major personal work acting either directly as the client or indirectly through observation and role playing. Many traumatic personal experiences were worked through; one student dealt with the loss of her baby; another dealt with a childhood sexual assault; and one student dealt with the immense burden resulting from an abusive relationship with her spouse.

Session Five: Letting Go

The fifth session was held in August about four months later. Initially, this session had been cancelled due to funding problems. However, the therapist, Dennis Knauert, volunteered to honour his commitment, at his own expense, and travelled from Thunder Bay, Ontario to work with our group. Because we had only one therapist for this session, we chose to focus on one theme. As many students had experienced a series of tragedies in each of their communities, we decided to focus on the aging, death, and grieving process. During the week the students shared losses that they were grieving. These losses included the recent death of a nephew in an auto accident and the suicide of one of our student's sons.

Session Six: Learning to Dance

Due to funding problems, the sixth personal development session was not held until the following June. It caused a disruption in the four-month cycle we had previously established. Many students were negatively affected by this break in rhythm. They felt let down and a sense of loss in missing the opportunity to deal, as a group, with issues that had arisen during the preceding months. Finally, in June, therapists Dennis Knauert and Nancy Fraser were hired to facilitate the session. This week was processed in a large group. Again, preparatory exercises lead up to students working individually on past traumas. Most of the work entailed family reconstruction and sculpturing. It was here that students witnessed the third and fourth generation transmission of grief, loss, and shame as well as the devastating impact alcoholism and the residential schools have had on their people. It was an extremely powerful week. It actively integrated into the students' lives many of the concepts and historical events learned during the past year.

Session Seven: Finding a Song

Because it was the last personal development session, we decided to hold a culturally-oriented retreat at the local treatment centre. We were honoured to have Dennis Knauert and Dr. Pam Colorado collaborate with us on this event. The purpose of this last session was to integrate the students' cultural strengths into their lives and help them rediscover their identities as Native people. The week began with a circle and the lighting of a sacred fire. This fire was maintained by the students throughout the week, except when group was in session. Then it was my responsibility to keep the fire burning. At particularly painful times, tobacco was offered to the fire to assist the students and the facilitators.

We found that intensive sessions occurred not only during the day, but also among the students themselves at night around the fire. Some experienced a profound sense of grief when they touched upon the loss of their culture. Other individual issues were again explored during the later stages of the week. In contrast to past sessions however, all of the work was done within the confines of the sacred circle and following morning prayers and smudging.

In this last session, students were asked to complete a chronology of the significant events that occurred during the past seven generations and then to envision what their families would be like seven generations from now. During one of our frequent treks into the bush, students were asked to select a "talking" stick. This stick would represent their families over the past and future generations. These sticks were then used in the same way as in art work to explore important issues. The profound spiritual context of this work led to remarkable insights among the students. The week ended with a field trip to the nearest mountain for a communal offering of tobacco and ribbons.

For me, one of my most powerful experiences came from playing the role of a student's father in one of the family sculptures. This man had been cited as an important helper to the great prophet Nogha many years before. However he had lost much of the meaning in his life through the death of many of his relatives, including his wife. No one in his family could bring him out of his profound grief and alcoholism until, one day, he was asked to teach his traditional knowledge to his grandson. It was at this point that he found the strength to stand again.

The Transformation

These personal development sessions had several important impacts. First, they helped students deal with their personal issues. As the program continued, students became more self-aware and were able to observe their own behaviours and coping mechanisms. Combined with the family of origin work done in the Family Dynamics course, students not only gained an awareness of their heritage, but they also observed the impact major events had had on their family systems during the family reconstruction and sculpturing sessions.

Second, when students understood each other on a more intimate level, they were better able to support and accept each other. For a number of students, it was the personal development and support provided by the Program and the resulting personal sense of growth that empowered them. Although a few found the level of intimacy that developed inside the student community threatening, most found themselves able to share experiences and feelings they would never have risked sharing before.

Third, by exploring personal histories, and by playing different family roles, students became more aware of their own, their family's, and their fellow students' issues. As a result, they gained greater insight into the problems and needs of their clients and their communities. For example, by playing the role of a sexually abused child, one student experienced the profound sense of shame and guilt the other suffered. By playing the role of an abusive husband, another student discovered the feeling of powerlessness and desperation the other felt. Most often, students touched the grief that resulted from the tremendous losses experienced within their families.

Fourth, the therapists were able to model sound clinical practice so that the students could observe a respectful and effective therapeutic process in action. They received direct, personal experience with a meaningful, powerful, and effective therapeutic relationship. Through these personal insights, they gained confidence and hope in what a therapeutic relationship could offer other family and community members.

Fifth, these sessions provided an excellent means of integrating theory and practice. Through dealing with various traumatic personal events, the students gained a deeper sense of the impact such events can have. This experience enabled them to empathize with clients who present similar issues. Although 15 class days of the Methods course are devoted to family violence and child abuse, in the personal development sessions, the students observed, and in some cases, experienced those events themselves.

Sixth, as Freire (1985) notes, true education allows students to question the status quo and reality as dictated by others. In this program, our students were among the first people in their communities to gain an awareness of the impact the colonial process has had on their families and communities. Some realized that it is no longer the missionary or the Indian agent who is responsible for the oppression of their people. That oppression has been internalized, and it is their own people, and in some cases, their own family members who perpetuate the long-standing tradition of dehumanization and cultural genocide. This revelation led to a great deal of conflict during the second year of the program. Some students criticized their supervisors, Band administrators, and Council members. Some politicians blamed me and the program for stirring up all this trouble and stated that "we should be training these students to become social workers not politicians." Subsequently, two of our students were among the 42 people nominated for election to the Dene Tha First Nation Council.

Many Native people have been empowered through the affirmation of their traditional values and helping skills. Through this program, our Native social work students had the opportunity to develop a helping style that best suits them and their communities.

Another result of this program was the transformation that occurred in the relationship between the students and the instructors. This relationship became one of interdependency, where all participants were enriched and empowered through their contact with each other. During the second year of the program, we were honoured to have instructors who were receptive to the knowledge and expertise of the Native students. Several instructors commented that they learned as much from the students as the students learned from them.

Finally, many of our students rediscovered or enhanced their identities as Native people. Many re-established a profoundly spiritual relationship with their grandparents, the land, and all living things. Although every student has a story to tell about the personal growth aspect of the Program, one of the most dramatic stories involved our oldest student. At the beginning of the program, Mary Francis described herself as a turtle. Her last formal educational experience had been in a residential school 40 years earlier. Returning to school had been a lifelong dream for Mary, and at age 57, she entered our Social Work Program. Throughout the first year Mary remained in her shell. Although she provided support for many of the younger students, she never saw herself as an Elder. During the Methods II course however, Mary's knowledge and skills in the traditional helping processes were acknowledged and valued. Mary came out of her shell and began to share a great deal of herself with others. She was instrumental in supporting the work of Dr. Colorado. In fact, Mary was later asked to participate in an international exchange of Elders at the San Francisco-based World Wide Indigenous Science Network. Mary became a valued resource person for all the field placement agencies she worked with, and she advised supervisors on appropriate ways of working with their Native clients. As the acknowledged class Elder, Mary led our morning circles and sweet grass ceremonies for the final stages of the Program.

Program Implications

Although innumerable implications can be drawn from this experience, several important items must be noted. First, social work educators can choose which road they want to follow in terms of training Native social workers. The old and familiar road is to continue the colonial process and train Native students in only the Western way of helping. However, by doing so, these educators continue the missionization and alienation of Native students from themselves. As we learned long ago, much is lost through this type of relationship. I believe that there is another road to successfully train social workers. This path challenges both students and instructors to approach each other with respect, and it offers Native students a balance of Western and traditional Native approaches to helping. Although all participants, Native and non-Native alike, will find this road more challenging and painful, I believe that everyone will be transformed and enriched by the experience.

Second, social work training programs have a tremendous impact not only on the student but also on the student's family. As the student grows, a shift occurs in the balance that exists in both situations. Depending upon the flexibility and health of the relationships among family members, the student's growth may lead to an enrichment of these intrafamilial relationships, or conversely, to crisis and potential family breakdown. For these reasons, spouses and significant others in the student's family must be considered in the development of support systems and the program orientation process.

Third, outreach programs have a tremendous impact on the community. In addition to the impact students will have on the agencies in which they are placed, their new sense of empowerment often leads to their questioning the relationships and power structures in the community. In small Native communities, this awakening can work both for and against the change process. For these reasons, local political leaders also need to be involved in the program orientation.

Fourth, in outreach programs, especially in the context of relatively small Native constituencies, the students reflect both the families and the communities to be served. Their personal issues represent an accurate cross-section of the problems likely to be encountered in their communities.

Fifth, intensive personal development sessions provide students an opportunity to deal with the issues that they bring to the program or will encounter during class or field placements. By successfully dealing with their own issues, students gain confidence in the therapeutic process and are better able to help their clients.

Sixth, in the context of Native students, personal development also involves the enhancement of their cultural and spiritual identities. Because this process occurs each day of class, Native instructors and Elders must be actively engaged in the program.

Over the course of this two-year program, I was honoured to witness the growth and development of these students. For many, the journey was difficult. Nearly all of the students had experienced personal crises, loss of relatives, and the stress of making new adjustments. Most painful for some was the realization of what they, as Native people, had lost. Within the context of their development as helping professionals, these students have gained a heightened awareness of their cultural identity as well as an appreciation of the strengths of their families and communities. They also have a better under-standing of their history and heritage. As the program came to a close, all of the students came together in the circle. Their songs and dreams will be carried by their children and grandchildren, and they will become the legends that future generations will call on for strength and guidance.

References

Freire, P. (1985). *Pedagogy of the oppressed.* New York, NY: Continuum Publishing.

Moore, P. & Wheelock, A. (1990). *Wolverine myths and visions.* Edmonton, AB: University of Alberta Press.

Pincus, A. & Minahan, A. (1973). *Social work practice: Model and method.* Itasca, IL: Peacock Press.

Chapter 12

The Blue Quills Experience

An interview with Doug Smith

David Hannis

In 1983, Doug Smith left a secure government social work position to become the first Coordinator of the Grant MacEwan Community College (GMCC) Social Work Program at Blue Quills First Nations College, which is located in St. Paul, Alberta, about 150 kilometers northeast of Edmonton. In this interview with David Hannis, Doug describes his seven years at Blue Quills and tells us what he learned from those experiences.

David Hannis (DH): *Doug, can you describe some of the history of Blue Quills prior to your being hired?*

Doug Smith (DS): Blue Quills College is a former residential school, which is now run by local aboriginal organizations. Since 1975, it had offered a number of experimental post-secondary programs at different times, including "Project Morning Star," a Bachelor of Education

(BEd) program offered in conjunction with the University of Alberta; and a Bachelor of Social Work (BSW) program offered in conjunction with the University of Calgary. Both of those programs had ended by the time I arrived in St. Paul. The problem with those programs was that they were offered at the university level, even though most of the local Native people seeking a post-secondary education at that time had not completed grade 12. Indeed, some had barely completed grade 8. The community college programs which we subsequently instigated provided an appropriate alternative to wholesale upgrading, and served as a necessary bridge between high school and university. At Blue Quills, classes were kept fairly small at around 20 to 25 participants, and this arrangement allowed for more personal interaction between instructors and students.

Initially, funding for the Grant MacEwan Community College program at St. Paul was only for the first year of a two-year program. This partial funding created a great deal of uncertainty, and we were pleased when it was subsequently extended to cover the full two years. As a result of being hired several months before courses began, I was able to orient myself to the community and got to know the potential students before classes commenced. This early exposure proved to be invaluable. I gained an appreciation of their difficulties, and at the same time, it allowed them to articulate their expectations of their new coordinator.

DH: *I understand that GMCC had tried unsuccessfully to establish a social work program at Blue Quills a year or so before you arrived. Why do you think this earlier attempt failed?*

DS: There were a number of problems, but the main one seemed to be that the program was offered only on a part-time basis, which meant that students sometimes had difficulties completing their assignments and meeting the expectations of their employers. Also, some of these students held powerful positions in their communities, and they were reluctant to accept the authority of non-aboriginal instructors.

DH: *What prompted your decision to leave a secure government job to become the Coordinator of the Social Work Program at Blue Quills?*

DS: There were a number of reasons. One was the potential I saw for education to break the "Welfare Cycle" that many of my social assistance clients were trapped in. To my disappointment and frustration, I discovered that post-secondary education could also become another form of "welfare." Therefore, when screening applicants, it was important to assess their motivation for seeking further education. We didn't want people who were going to treat the program as another meaningless "make-work" project or who were only going to attend so that they could pick up their cheques. We sought people who had a sincere desire to go into social work; people who wanted to help others as well as themselves. The successful applicants were those who saw that the program offered them an opportunity to gain power, to achieve mobility, to make choices, and to attain something that would make a difference to their lives.

DH: *How did you identify the successful applicants, and what did you observe about the people who applied for the program?*

DS: Most of the Native students (we also had some non-aboriginal adult learners in our program) had poor reading and writing skills. Cree was usually their first language. Cree is a picture language; it is rarely written down. Since it is such a descriptive language, it was sometimes difficult for aboriginal students to conceptualize in English. Most of our students were older women who had been helpers in the past, and several had nursing backgrounds. As the program proceeded, the number of non-aboriginals who applied to this Indian Affairs-funded program increased substantially, which made the applicant selection even more difficult. In our first two-year program, about 20% of the students were non-Native.

DH: *How was your role as program coordinator defined?*

DS: As the program became established, it grew from a one-year to a full two-year program, which was subsequently repeated several times. As the program developed, my role became more clearly defined. Since I lived in St. Paul, it was difficult to remain completely detached and objective about the needs of the people there. Fortunately, however, I did not become too embroiled in the local issues. Rather, I saw my role to be that of an interpreter and a bridge between Grant MacEwan's Social Work program and the Blue Quills community. I was the administrator of the program as well as the supervisor of field placements.

The great pacifiers of anxieties on both sides were the instructors who came from Edmonton. They would come to the St. Paul campus, and after a time, our apprehensive students would say, "they're okay." At the end of their courses, the equally apprehensive instructors would go back to Edmonton and say the same thing. Students would ask the Edmonton instructors what they did differently on the Edmonton campus. Invariably, they would reply, "nothing." The students appreciated that.

I often spent time with these instructors in a kind of peer-teaching situation. I tried to meet their needs so that all they had to do was teach, mark, and submit grades. In this way, the instructors were protected from local politics and other distractions. As a result, I never had to pressure instructors to come to Blue Quills. They came to teach, not just for the money, but also for the experience. When the President of the College, the Dean of the Arts and Sciences Division, the Dean of Community Services, and the Chair of the Social Work Program personally visited Blue Quills, it sent a message to the students that they were valued and that my activities as coordinator were recognized. Part of my role as coordinator was to provide a unique, supportive, and personal environment in which students could learn. On the other hand, because the environment was somewhat artificial and protected, it made the subsequent task of adjusting to life at university more difficult for those students who chose to continue their education at the University of Calgary.

DH: *Most of your instructors came from Edmonton where they had experience teaching these courses on the main campus. Did you try to recruit any local instructors?*

DS: We tried, but most of the suitably qualified local people already had full time jobs. They were willing to teach in the evening, but the majority of our students had family commitments, which meant they could attend day classes only. However, we did ask local trainers from Native Counselling Services to deliver specific modules of the Family Dynamics course. We also hired local professionals to facilitate suicide prevention classes and workshops on addictions. These people brought a practical perspective to the program, and their presence in the classroom helped build bridges between our program and prospective local employers.

DH: *In what ways did the students themselves change while they were in the program?*

DS: In addition to wanting to help others, many students attended our social work program because it provided them with an opportunity to address their own personal problems. This program confirmed the old adage that you cannot help anyone else until you have taken care of yourself. When Kay Feehan, the Program's Chairperson, came to the Integration Seminar and talked about rural social work she told the students, "You are your best resource," and "You know a lot more than you think you know." The students knew what she meant and knew it was not just lip service. You can only take the client as far as you've gone yourself. Those who made it to the end of the two years gradually sorted out a lot of things in their own lives along the way. They cut out the drinking; they dealt with abusive and unhelpful spouses; they tried to break the cycle of violence and addiction; and, they owned up to personal issues such as being the child of an alcoholic parent. The students learned some steps from the social work methods courses that they immediately applied to their personal and professional lives. They were also able to assess whether or not their own life experiences were a help or a hindrance to the helping process.

DH: *What was your role in assisting students with their personal growth?*

DS: The first Personal Growth course, although helpful, was not long enough, and as the program proceeded, problems arose with respect to attitudes, behaviours, and personality conflicts. It became obvious that we needed to address these issues on a regular, ongoing basis if our students were to succeed. Consequently, additional time was built into the program. Each week, between clusters of courses, and at the end and beginning of trimesters, special sessions were held to address personal and interpersonal concerns. Outside facilitators were sometimes brought in to lead these sessions. However, the decision to screen out inappropriate students remained mine, which was always very difficult for me. I did, however, notice that many of the students who were asked to leave the program often appeared relieved.

It was always difficult to get funding for these personal development courses because it was virtually impossible to measure their success in tangible ways. So, the more courses we did, the more creative we became. I myself participated in one personal growth workshop, which despite my initial apprehension, proved to be an invaluable experience for me.

DH: *Your program's admission criteria was the same as that used to admit students to the social work program on the Edmonton campus. What were some of the reasons students dropped out of your program, and approximately what proportion of the total student body did they represent?*

DS: Our drop-out rate was about 10% to 25%, probably higher than in Edmonton. Most students dropped out because they were unable to complete assignments. Because our classes were smaller, the impact of dropouts was noticeably felt by everyone. When someone left the program, his or her classroom chair always remained empty, and no one would ever sit in that particular spot.

DH: *St. Paul is about 150 kilometers from Edmonton, and instructors from the city usually came to teach for a week at a time. Given the need to condense courses into such relatively short time frames, do you think the program offered at Blue Quills was as good as the one in Edmonton, where courses are taught over a 15-week period, where access to libraries and other resources is easier, and where there is a greater choice of field placements?*

DS: Our library was quite good. We inherited a lot of books from the old residential school as well as those that were left over from previous university courses. In addition, we carefully reviewed the course bibliographies, sometimes with the instructors, and purchased all the essential texts. We also borrowed a lot of books from the main campus in Edmonton and from other college libraries. I also loaned or donated many of my own books.

We had fewer problems with respect to library resources than we did with field placements. Many of the practicum supervisors had no formal credentials, and consequently I had to intervene more directly with training the trainers than perhaps would have been the case in Edmonton. However, we were always conscious of maintaining standards and not offering a "watered down" program.

DH: *How did you address the issue of culturally relevant curricula?*

DS: Generally, our instructors were very good at tailoring their materials to meet student needs, and usually it was not an issue. In any case, our students wanted to know what the rest of the world was like. For instance, it was helpful for students to find out that wife battering was not just an aboriginal problem.

The program also provided one of the few opportunities for aboriginals and non-Natives to talk meaningfully with each other. I was speaking with a Native woman in my office one day, and she told me that it was one of the few times she had ever spoken to a white man outside of a bar. That discussion did more to promote healthy aboriginal/non-aboriginal understanding than any Native awareness workshop could have done.

Most students did not want to be treated differently because they were aboriginal. They simply wanted their social work colleagues, Native and non-Native alike, to treat them as competent professionals. In the process of gaining social work skills, many of our aboriginal students also learned more about their own cultural identity. For example, one Native student told me that, after two years, she had finally found out from a white person what an Indian was.

DH: *You saw many instructors come and go while you were at Blue Quills. What did you observe about the most successful ones?*

DS: The most effective instructors were the ones who knew their material; who could teach without referring to textbooks; who didn't need a lot of overheads or equipment; and, who didn't become immobilized when the taperecorder, VCR, or film projector broke down. They were flexible, approachable people who were willing to abandon lesson plans that were obviously not working, and who were willing to spend time getting to know their students. The most successful instructors understood and sympathized when students did not attend class because a relative had died; they were willing to go that extra mile for their students.

DH: *What were relations like in the classroom between the aboriginal and non-aboriginal students?*

DS: Resentment frequently revolved around funding issues. Aboriginal students were often perceived as being treated more favourably because their education was being paid for by the Department of Indian Affairs and Northern Development. Grades were more important to the non-Native students. They resented any classroom behaviors, such as non-attendance, which might affect group project marks. Classes tended to move at the pace of the slowest learner. I discouraged class voting, and instead, promoted consensus decision-making to address periodic conflicts. Competition was de-emphasized and collaborative efforts encouraged.

Some aboriginal students considered themselves to be at a disadvantage when an instructor's question was not put directly to them but rather presented to the entire class. This situation was a cultural issue. Three aboriginal students came to my office one day and said, "We're never going to be able to compete. We're always going to be described as shy and quiet because we only speak if a question is directed to us. You know what it's like in that classroom. You throw out a question like it was basketball, and all the non-aboriginal students leap to grab the thing, while the aboriginal students sit and wait!" If instructors hope to involve aboriginal students in classroom discussions they must learn to ask each student personally what he or she thinks about an issue. Native students won't interrupt instructors, out of respect, and if instructors respect their students, then they must adapt their communication style and ask students individually for a response.

I used to tell students that they may have to change some of their ideas if they are going to be heard in the wider world. "You are not losing a cultural value," I used to say, "but are learning how to survive in another world." To compensate for this cultural difference, they would sometimes select a spokesperson to answer for them in class. On one occasion, I asked a student in class if she was speaking for the group or for herself and she replied, "For the group." I then asked her how she knew that; did they pass her notes or something? She answered that it was a kind of "telepathy!" I told them that this aspect of aboriginal culture could really interfere with some students' learning. I suggested that as future leaders they might one day be sitting down at the negotiating table with the Government of Canada. To be effective there, they would have to learn to be more direct, more assertive.

DH: *Knowing what you know now, if you were to go back to 1983 and start all over again, what would you do differently?*

DS: I would not go to a rural community owning an import car, where there are no dealerships or places to have the car serviced. Seriously, I came to Blue Quills at a time when change was possible. For the longest while, I worried about doing the right thing rather than accepting that I was doing the best I could, and that maybe no one knew what the "right thing" was. We were all breaking new ground. I recall one incident where a sociology instructor was unable to complete his course, and on the day of his last scheduled class, I had to go to a meeting in Edmonton. Meanwhile, the students had prepared their class presentations, which would affect their final marks. What should I do? There was no precedent for this situation. I decided to relinquish control and to trust the students. They did not abuse that trust. For six gruelling hours, they worked through their class presentations and submitted themselves to peer review. Their written work was then reviewed by instructors in Edmonton.

In hindsight, there were some minor things I could have done differently, but the basic learning experience was there. The fact that the students didn't take off, on that last day, as soon as my car was out of sight was a measure of their commitment to their learning and to their new profession. Our program was successful because it had four essential components: personal development, social work theory, hands-on experience, and academic courses. The fact that the program was transferable to university was also an important aspect.

DH: *Did students in the Blue Quills program ever experience difficulties in their personal relationships while taking the course?*

DS: Yes. A little learning can cause a lot of change. As students gained new knowledge and developed their assessment skills, they began to look at their relationships in new ways. I had more than one irate husband in my office challenging me on what we were teaching in our courses.

Because some students lived in oppressive relationships, discussions on gender inequities, for example, had a certain poignancy. And when you are a rape victim, discussions on sexual abuse become more than an academic exercise.

To go back to your earlier question, in hindsight, I do not think I would have done anything differently. Every situation was unique. Some of the things I did were responses to different students, different needs, and different situations. I was in a good place to learn how to deal with secrets, one of which was my own Multiple Sclerosis.

DH: *What has happened to your former students?*

DS: Two or three have gone on to university and have done well there. The rest are doing what they entered the program to learn. Some work on various reserves and in non-aboriginal social service agencies, in schools, in addiction centres, in women's shelters, and so forth. Some of those who dropped out of the Blue Quills program later finished the program in Edmonton. Of the first eight who graduated, one has died, and the remaining seven are still employed. Most of the other graduates are working where they had hoped to work, and a couple have entered the political arena.

DH: *Do you feel that the graduates who are working now are more effective helpers because they have a Diploma in Social Work?*

DS: Yes. Based on my discussions with graduates, I think they know more. They have a broader perspective. Because they know more, the work is harder for them. They are more self-reliant. They have some social work methods skills and community development skills. A former student, who has been working for a few years, said to me, "I should be burnt out. It is this community which needs to heal itself, not me. When this thing (crisis) was going down, it suddenly occurred to me the different roles I had to play. I remembered the group work course, the community practice course, and the methods course." When graduates make these kinds of statements and tell me that they are applying the skills they learned at our

College in their own communities, and when they tell me they are less afraid of the future, I know that we must have done something right.

This interview was conducted in Edmonton at the end of 1992. Doug Smith has since left Grant MacEwan Community College for health reasons. After his retirement, he received the Grant MacEwan Outstanding Employee Medallion in recognition of his contributions to the College.

Chapter 13

Evaluating Excellence

What the research has told us

David Hannis

Someone once said, "Words don't matter; people do." Most social workers believe this adage and often resist attempts made by "number crunchers" to reduce clients to mere statistics. While these sentiments are admirable and such scepticism is healthy, social workers sometimes rely too heavily on intuition and subjective knowledge and fail to recognize the limitations of these approaches. We forget that not everyone thinks like us. As a result, we often neglect, at the outset, the systematic recording of data that could be useful to subsequent program evaluators. When this benign neglect is combined with the difficulty of accurately assessing such intangibles as personal growth and professional competence, reliable program evaluations become even more of a challenge.

Despite these limitations, most of Grant MacEwan Community College's (GMCC) Social Work Outreach programs have been the subject of independent scrutiny which has yielded much useful information. Based on the subjective observations of community leaders, students, instructors, employers, and administrators, the research that has been done has indicated that GMCC's programs have been quite successful at achieving goals. While outreach program costs and attrition rates have typically been higher than on-campus programs, closer inspection of the data reveals that a careful cost-benefit analysis must include consideration of other variables besides the mere numbers of successful graduates. The employment placement record of these social work graduates has been very good, with most of them opting to remain in their home areas. These outreach programs have been quite successful therefore in producing social workers who are sensitive to both local conditions and client needs.

From the very beginning, GMCC has insisted on independent evaluations of its Social Work programs for aboriginal people; (Kuwada's study was the first, completed in 1979). Later, Audrey McLaughlin evaluated three of GMCC's programs before becoming the leader of Canada's Federal New Democratic Party.

These independent studies opened GMCC's Social Work programs to public scrutiny and yielded data, which both satisfied funders and suggested areas for improvement. As a result, ongoing fine-tuning of GMCC's Social Work Outreach programs has been possible for the beginning which, in turn, has enhanced the effectiveness of subsequent programs. Although the studies confirmed that attrition rates were higher in these outreach programs, they remained, nevertheless, at acceptable levels. Moreover, some of the students who "dropped out" later resumed their studies and subsequently graduated.

Costs per student have also been criticized, and it is true that it is more expensive to deliver a two-year program in a rural location than it is in a large urban center like Edmonton. Rural class sizes are frequently (but not always) smaller than on-campus programs, and substantial transportation and accommodation costs are incurred when most course instructors reside in Edmonton. Outreach courses also usually run longer, for 60 hours, as opposed to the normal 45-hours for city programs. This additional instructional time inevitably increases costs. The provision of extra personal development opportunities, the mileage expenses associated with on-site visits to field placement students, and the travel costs incurred when coordinators attend administrative meetings in Edmonton also add to program expenditures.

Audrey McLaughlin (1985) has pointed out another side to this cost equation. When calculating the expense of delivering a program, one must also take into account the expenditures associated with *not* providing such educational opportunities. Many Native communities today are in a fractured state. Although the recent improvements made on some reserves cannot be discounted, many aboriginal people continue to suffer from the effects of extreme deprivation, typically characterised by high levels of abuse and a sense of powerlessness. The majority of non-Native professionals who move into such communities are usually inexperienced, come from different cultural backgrounds, and invariably don't stay long. As any business person will testify, productivity suffers when the rate of worker turnover is high. Hiring local workers not only reduces the cost to employers, it also suggests that the quality of service provided is likely to be higher. At the same time, these newly trained, local professionals may inspire others to return to school to upgrade their skills and subsequently achieve gainful employment.

When the above factors are taken into consideration, calculating the cost of delivering aboriginal social work programs becomes more complicated than merely dividing the total budget by the number of students who have graduated. After these other variables have been considered, and when the cost of training one social worker is compared to the expense of educating other helping professionals, (a psychiatrist, for example) one begins to develop a better perspective on the situation (McLaughlin, 1984).

All of the Social Work program evaluations which have been completed have essentially been summative studies, conducted close to the end of each project. With "tight" budgets, thought is rarely given at the outset of most human service projects (including GMCC's outreach activities), to establishing procedures for the systematic gathering of qualitative data which would ultimately facilitate the assessment of program effectiveness. Pretest information, against which any subsequent program changes can be measured, is rarely available. (Although currently some initiatives are being taken in this area.) This oversight is not merely a reflection of the sceptical attitudes mentioned at the beginning of this chapter, but rather the difficulty of accurately assessing change in areas of human development. Adult learning is not always a continuous process, and even when change is obvious, it is not always possible to discount the influence of other variables. I know of many excellent projects that have foundered in the past simply because workers were unable to answer the one basic question funders always ask, "As a result of your specific intervention, what undesirable events have you been able to prevent, or what desirable outcomes have you achieved?"

To accurately assess the effectiveness of GMCC's Social Work programs, the evaluation process would need to begin at an earlier stage and continue in an action research format throughout the duration of the project. This process would clearly add to the cost of delivering the programs and would probably not yield data substantially different to what we already know.

Despite these methodological limitations, the evaluations conducted on GMCC's Social Work programs have been helpful. One difficulty evaluators identified at an early stage related to the way these programs were funded. Initially, program funders (primarily the Department of Indian Affairs and Northern Development) were hesitant to commit funds beyond the first year of the two-year program. This hesitation produced some uncertainty and mistrust among aboriginal students and may have discouraged some eligible students from applying. Most of the students who were accepted into the program had family obligations that prevented them from transferring into the second year of the program on the main campus in Edmonton. Therefore, without long-term funding commitments, there was a good chance that some students would be "stranded" at the end of the first year of their studies with an unrecognized credential. The sponsors' reluctance to commit to long-term funding also created problems for program administrators who consequently had difficulties making informed decisions, planning course instructors' workloads, and assigning the most experienced teachers to outreach activities.

A second related issue was also identified by program evaluators. It concerned the communication difficulties among the various "players" in these programs including GMCC staff, federal civil servants, Band Councils, and members of the local educational institutions. As a result, the on-site GMCC program coordinator had to be extremely tolerant, adept at developing trust at a number of different levels, and skilled at handling conflict. Since the intent of the program was to empower students and bring about meaningful change, it was not therefore surprising for program coordinators to observe, and occasionally become embroiled in, disagreements with students, their families, and their communities. More than once, coordinators reported finding themselves blamed for the stressful new behaviors students were exhibiting at home, and moving testimonies by our graduates occasionally revealed the depth and intensity of the personal distress their studies had precipitated.

Providing personal development opportunities for students as well as offering ongoing emotional and practical support were identified as critical to the success of GMCC's Social Work programs. Most students were highly motivated to succeed; many travelled long distances over rural roads, sometimes in appalling weather, to get to class. Family demands did not cease when students enrolled in the program, nor did their community obligations, and these pressures often placed enormous strain on students and their families. Thus, the practical support provided by the program coordinators often became critical to students' success or failure. The expansion of the outreach course time from 45 to 60 hours was an acknowledgement that in-class time was needed for students to work on collaborative projects, to access scarce resources such as textbooks, to obtain personal support from instructors, and to be away from family and other distractions.

The evaluators also identified other pedagogical and curricular issues. Although frequent efforts were made to recruit local instructors sensitive to cultural issues, most course instructors were (and continue to be) non-Native and based in Edmonton. Many students came to the program with an incomplete secondary education and requiring some academic upgrading before beginning their social work training. Instructors who were sensitive to their students' needs and who took appropriate steps to build a healthy rapport with them were the most appreciated and the most successful. Students valued instructors' efforts to introduce a level of cultural relevance into their courses, although for a variety of reasons that task was sometimes difficult. At the same time, students were concerned that such course adaptations did not produce "watered-down" material or courses that were unduly focused on Native communities and ignored the broader societal picture. Alcoholism, drug abuse, family breakdown, neglect, mental illness, and deviancy are also features of "white" society, and frequently aboriginal students took some comfort in knowing this.

The teaching methodologies most instructors employed with their aboriginal students were primarily the same as those used with non-Native learners. All adult students, so theory and practice tells us, like to have their wisdom validated by the instructor. They frequently learn best by doing, and they often respond well to egalitarian classroom arrangements, where the line between teacher and student is less distinct. Success is more likely when both the teacher and the student are engaged in a process of "authentic dialogue," with both acting as critical co-investigators in search of truth (Freire 1981).

Field placement was another area of difficulty mentioned in some of the evaluations. In urban settings, social work practice is generally more specialized, and it is possible for a social worker to spend his or her entire day counselling. In rural areas, the workload is likely to be more eclectic. In addition to counselling, rural social work practice frequently involves identifying local support systems, facilitating the formation of self-help groups, undertaking educational presentations, making referrals, training volunteers, advising boards, writing funding proposals, helping to build effective organizations, assisting with community needs surveys, gathering information, liaising with other agencies, and briefing local leaders. In her Blue Quills study, McLaughlin (1985) noted that this rural/urban difference was not clearly acknowledged on the evaluation forms used to assess student competence in field practice settings. She also noted that there was not enough emphasis on the development of community practice skills in the social work outreach programs.

Related to curriculum and teaching practice issues is the question of standards. Program evaluators found no evidence that the courses delivered offcampus to aboriginal students were academically inferior or that different criteria was used to assess student competence. As mentioned earlier, most Native students are fiercely opposed to "watered-down" courses and want to be judged by the same criteria as their "white," urban counterparts. They want culturally relevant courses, not courses that are academically substandard. This expectation is particularly challenging for non-aboriginal instructors to address.

In reviewing the qualifications of the instructors who taught off campus, McLaughlin (1984) commented that they were "exceptionally well-qualified." The outreach instructors themselves reported that they set the same standards for their off-campus students as they did for those who attended classes in Edmonton.

Although library facilities are not as extensive in rural areas, and some field placement supervisors lack formal credentials, these factors did not appear to affect overall program quality. The staff of the GMCC Learning Resources Centre in Edmonton were acknowledged as being cooperative and efficient when dealing with outreach students' telephone requests for materials. The outreach instructors also made sure that relevant course materials were available in the off-campus classroom by the time they arrived.

The issue of field placement personnel having less formal training than their urban counterparts and not fully appreciating the complexities of student supervision is not unique to rural areas. There is not always a correlation between formal qualifications and competence. In the city, a close relationship often develops between instructors and field placement supervisors which ensures the maintenance of high quality learning environments. This collaborative relationship is supported by weekly integration seminars, regular agency visits, and training sessions for supervisors. In rural areas, the same model is generally followed, although the distances coordinators have to travel to visit field placement agencies are much greater.

Another area some of the evaluators investigated was the issue of student motivation. One of the questions explored was that of the student's perception of the program. Did they regard these programs as merely an extension of the "welfare cycle," or were they genuinely committed to work hard, to change, and to obtain gainful employment in their own communities upon graduation? Here the facts speak for themselves. First, an extensive orientation session is always given to potential students before actual social work courses begin. Not only do these pre-course classes provide opportunities for academic upgrading and personal development, they also provide instructors with an opportunity to assess students. These sessions give students a glimpse of what they are getting themselves into, and if necessary, an opportunity to screen themselves out. Even so, as already mentioned, attrition rates remain higher for these off-campus programs. At a 1988 conference on Native Education, two program coordinators offered some comments on this situation:

"Problems such as family responsibilities, family expectations, inadequate academic preparation, sometimes irrelevant curriculum, some students still in a client mode rather than potential helpers, and family and friends who feel threatened by education are real life issues faced by students. Success is increased when ownership and control are in Native hands, and when the programs are experiential; (spirituality is a vital component), (when) counselling and support is ongoing, and (when) there is adequate financing.

Grant MacEwan Community College, 1988

Given these realities, rather than concentrating on the issue of dropouts, perhaps we should "reframe" this concern by asking the more pertinent question: "Given the tremendous hardships associated with travelling long distances to attend classes and maintaining family and community obligations while studying, why isn't the attrition rate higher for these students?" Restivo (1990) noted that during the four years that GMCC offered the social work program through the Yellowhead Tribal Council near Edmonton, six students had babies, one student had two babies, and in order to continue in the program two other students, both pregnant, commuted weekly from their reserve, about 150 kilometres away.

Overall, the evaluations of GMCC's Social Work outreach programs for aboriginal students have been extremely positive. They report that important goals were met and that most graduates enhanced their employability and found jobs locally. The data also suggests that these graduates have been more effective in those jobs than they would have been without the diploma. A small number of program graduates have also gone on to university to attain their Bachelor of Social Work (BSW) degree. Some entered the University of Calgary's Social Work Program in Edmonton, while others enrolled in the all-Native BSW program delivered by the University of Calgary in conjunction with the Yellowhead Tribal Council. As a result, there is now a growing number of aboriginal social workers, trained at both the college and university level, who are working on reserves and in other settings throughout Alberta. Some of these GMCC graduates have told their stories elsewhere in this book (Beaulieu, 1993; Lalonde, 1993; Peacock, 1993). They have indicated that the transition from the relatively protected atmosphere of the college classroom to the university campus was not smooth, with grades typically dropping during the initial, emotionally-trying adaptation period. Undoubtedly, assigning someone who is sensitive to Native culture and the needs of adult learners to act as a mentor during these early days at university would help aboriginal students adjust more quickly and easily to the rigors of university life and retain some measure of their self-esteem.

Overall, despite some methodological limitations, the evaluations of GMCC's off-campus Social Work programs have yielded promising data. The appointment of a local on-site coordinator who is an efficient administrator, a good communicator, trustworthy, competent, compassionate, and culturally sensitive has proven to be vital component to the success of these programs. Having instructors with these same characteristics is also important. Adequate, assured, long-term funding is another key component of a successful program. Fostering collaborative working and teaching environments is also essential. Overall, attrition rates have been at acceptable levels and employment rates for graduates have been encouragingly high.

These evaluations have been extremely helpful. To conduct more comprehensive studies would require more time, more sophisticated survey instruments, and of course, more money. Even with more detailed, "objective" evaluation systems in place, it's debateable if we would learn anything more than we already intuitively seem to know, that is, that GMCC's Social Work outreach programs for aboriginal students have been an unqualified success.

References

Freire, P. (1981). *Pedagogy of the oppressed.* New York: Heider and Heider.

Grant MacEwan Community College (1988). *Our people; our struggles; our spirit.* A conference on Native education. Conference summary. Edmonton, AB: GMCC.

Kuwada, T. (1979). *Final report Native Social Services Worker Program, Grant MacEwan College.* Edmonton, AB: GMCC.

McLaughlin, A. (1980). *Evaluation, Native Social Services Worker Program (Yukon), Grant MacEwan Community College.* Edmonton, AB: GMCC.

McLaughlin, A. (1984). *Evaluation, of the Social Services Worker Outreach Program, year 1, Slave Lake, Alberta.* Edmonton, AB: GMCC.

McLaughlin, A. (1985). *Interim report, evaluation of the Social Services Worker Program, Grant MacEwan Community College, Blue Quills Native Education Centre.* Edmonton, AB: GMCC.

Restivo, G. (1990). *Yellowhead Tribal Council, GMCC, Social Work Program, Spruce Grove, four-year program report (1986-1990).* Edmonton, AB: GMCC.

Chapter 14

Walking in Two Worlds

Restivo • Peacock • Beaulieu • Lalonde

The Power of Healing

By Gino Restivo

The sweet scent of sage permeates the room as the Elder prepares for the healing ceremony. Inside the circle of life he prays to the Creator as his assistant offers sweetgrass to all the participants. After the smudging and prayer, the participants hug each other warmly and prepare themselves for the Elder's teachings. The Elder speaks of the importance of being balanced and of how we must learn to face the darkness of our existence.

Suddenly, a lady falls to the ground. The Elder instructs the group to form a close circle around her. He reaches for his blanket and medicines and begins a hypnotic, mystical healing chant. He covers the woman with the blanket and applies various sacred herbs. The Elder continues his chant as he strikes her back, as if attempting to expel the poison within her.

The woman's scream is piercing, almost non-human. As the other participants sway to and fro, their tears of silence reveal the unspoken truth of their existence as Native people. Colonization, oppression, persecution, and cultural, spiritual, social, economic and political genocide have lead to unprecedented levels of alcoholism, suicide, poverty and de-humanization, and physical, emotional, and sexual abuse.

The Elder continues to pray and eventually, the woman's horrifying screams end. The participants are told to lay their hands on her back. The blanket is removed, and they welcome her back with hugs and reassurances. As she re-enters the circle, the Elder passes around the feather. Some speak openly, others cry in silence, and others quickly pass the feather on for fear that their darkness may engulf them. The circle ends with the Elder again stressing the importance of living a balanced life, and he breaks the circle with a prayer.

This short vignette is an example of the powerful healing that is happening among Native people today. The unusual thing about this particular event was that it occurred during a Social Work Outreach Program delivered by Grant MacEwan Community College (GMCC). It is one example of the culturally appropriate, experiential learning that GMCC has pioneered and integrated into many of its outreach programs. The administrators of the GMCC Social Work Program believe that healing oneself is an essential component in the process of healing others. This program is designed to facilitate personal growth. Classes are longer and more attention is given to personal and group development. Most of the instructors are skilled counsellors or clinicians with extensive training in human development and adult education.

In the Native-oriented social work programs, much time is spent on addressing the symptomatic manifestations of colonization. Through role plays, family genograms, field practicums, and healing circles, students learn to face the horrors of their community's past existence. Some become totally immobilized and some become enraged, but most of the students experience a new way of being; an existence that demands empowerment and freedom from oppression and racial entrapment. They begin to recognize their own power and begin to take control of their own lives. This new ability has a profound effect on their families, their friends, and their communities. They have become part of a healing movement that will dramatically change the future of their nation.

The GMCC Social Work Program helps Native students to discover new paths to empowerment. The Native studies and cultural components of the program provide students with the cultural knowledge necessary for identity restructuring. By integrating traditional Native values with social work principles, students develop the tools they need to function within two worlds. As one Elder beautifully expressed it, "the student learns to walk in both worlds with one spirit."

Growing Together and Finding the Balance

by Carolyn Peacock

It is a great privilege to be asked to share some of my memories and experiences as a former student of the Grant MacEwan Community College Social Work Diploma Program. I was one of 18 graduates from the first Yellowhead Tribal Council (YTC)/Grant MacEwan Community College (GMCC) two-year Social Work Program in 1988. I would like to dedicate these memories and experiences to two special people who were involved in that program—a classmate, Dorothy Ward, and an instructor, John Hutton. Both of these people gave so much to us in their own unique ways. They were our friends and role models, and we all miss them dearly.

In 1986, the five YTC Chiefs signed a Dual Bilateral Child Welfare Agreement with the Federal and the Alberta governments. The Yellowhead Tribal Services Agency was also formed at that time to deliver child welfare services to its member Bands. With this agency in mind, the first two-year Social Work Program was developed. From the outset it was the vision of all the people involved in setting up this program to prepare students to return to their respective communities after graduation to facilitate the move toward local control of the Child Welfare programs. Consequently, everyone's expectations were high. As students, we felt responsible for the success or failure of this program.

As students and individuals, we had to make many adjustments while attending the program. The majority of our class was comprised of women, all of whom had children and had been out of school for some time. Only a few of us had graduated from high school and fewer still had any post secondary education. Therefore, entering the program and making a two-year commitment to obtain a Social Work Diploma was a huge step for many of us to take. We were fortunate that a major portion of our program focused on personal development. In retrospect, I personally believe that this component was one of the major contributors to the success of our program. It brought us together as a group; it helped us to deal individually with personal issues; and for many of us, it was a starting point in the healing process. A special bond developed among our group members, and it was the seed from which many close friendships grew. Our first personal development instructor was Juliana Kratz. She gave us the beautiful gift of a theme song called *We Are The World.* The words in this song summed up the thoughts and feelings of our class. Although we were unsure of our future, we all wanted to change and make a difference, both individually and collectively. The first time it was played, we stood in a circle, held hands, and cried with uncertainty. Over the next two years, that song was our motivator; it helped us to realize that we could accomplish our goals. The song was played again at our graduation and last day together, but on that occasion our tears were tears of joy. We cried because we were finished; we had graduated and were now going our separate ways. We were a strong group of women who would continue to contribute to our communities. Some went back to their Bands to work in the Child Welfare Programs, in Income Security, in drug and alcohol abuse programs, and as school counsellors. Others, like myself, went on to university to obtain their Bachelor of Social Work degree. The majority of these graduates pursued careers in social work.

I believe that, as students, we took ownership of the program and determined how we could make our learning meet our needs. We elected a student council, set up our own coffee fund, and organized student outings. Gino Restivo, our coordinator, counsellor, and friend, encouraged us to be the authors of our own development and the development of our group.

Numerous contributions to the personal development aspect of our program were made by our instructors, practicum supervisors, and members of the Yellowhead Tribal Council. They organized group activities, get-togethers, a family day, and two class retreats. They arranged funding for us to attend two Child Welfare Conferences. All of this support came at times when we needed the motivation to continue on with our studies.

All of our courses were challenges; the content and the tasks involved were not easy. We had to work hard to get through each and every class. It was all new territory for many of us. In order to process all of this new information, we had study groups, tutoring sessions, and class discussions to help us connect personal experiences with the concepts we were learning. For a number of the students, the most difficult part of the program was the written work. English was their second language and not commonly spoken in the home. Their frames of reference were based on the Cree, Saulteaux, and Stony languages. Many English words cannot be translated into these languages.

Watching the personal growth and development of all of these students was incredible. Each and every one of us grew and blossomed into strong and beautiful individuals. One student was so shy, she could not speak in class when asked. At the beginning of the two-year program, she would start to cry every time she attempted to share her thoughts and feelings. By the end of the program, she was able to speak confidently, without crying, and she presented herself very well. She was our most conspicuous flower.

In order to grow, we all had to share some very personal and painful experiences that we had never discussed with anyone before. We had to learn to trust and support one another. Many times it was extremely painful to hear what our classmates had been through or were still struggling with. As a class, we dealt with social issues that ranged from alcoholism, sexual abuse, and family violence to divorce, suicide, and ungrieved death. We were all survivors on the road to becoming healthy social workers.

Another important aspect of the program's personal growth and development component involved Indian culture and spirituality. We were fortunate to have Native Elders and spiritual advisors who worked with us on both a group and an individual basis. For me, this component formed the balance between the two worlds in which I lived and learned. The values we were taught helped us to heal both spiritually and emotionally, and at the same time, gave us the strength to continue healing, growing, and learning.

As a class, we dealt with all kinds of traumatic situations on a weekly basis. That was our reality. During our two years together, I believe each of us had to face some kind of crisis. It was normal for us to provide moral support for each other; we became a family. When something happened to one person, it affected all of us, our instructors included. Over the course of our program we dealt with the following personal crises: deaths of family members, family breakups, financial hardships, serious car accidents, serious illnesses, political changes in our communities, and personal separations from families and friends. Even though we tried hard to provide each other with personal support and counselling, we still had four students drop out during the first year and nine students drop out in the second year. We had to juggle our everyday lives in order to succeed. The mothers and wives had to study, do assignments, and at the same time, maintain their home life. During the day, we went to class; at night, we went home, did our housework, mothering, and everything else with our families. It was especially hard to leave home when our children were sick or when other family issues arose, but we could not miss classes. It was one of the painful sacrifices we had to make in order to accomplish our goals. During the course, two students gave birth, and both women returned to classes shortly thereafter. During especially tough times, one of the things that helped us was the humor. We were able to joke and laugh with one another and have a good time; it was our therapy.

Personally speaking, this program was one of the best things that ever happened to me. It came at a crucial point in my life. I needed a career change, and I was grieving a job in which I had invested ten years of my life. The Social Work Program helped me to resolve many personal issues and to develop professionally.

Despite the fact the course content was very challenging, I believed that I could be a social worker. It was only after I read the *Social Work Code of Ethics* that I realized what I was committing myself to. I felt that this document aptly summarized what social work was all about. I remember thinking, how am I going to learn everything I need to know in order to be able to do all of the things a social worker does? Will I be able to remember all that I have learned to work with people effectively and to do the best that I can for them?

I think what I liked best about our social work classes was the "hands on" experience we received. The focus was not solely on the academic side of social work; we were able to connect academic theory to practical experience. All of our instructors took the time to work with each of us individually. They were constantly checking up on us to see if we were having difficulties. As a student, the hardest area for me was learning about the larger social work issues and associating what I was learning with the "big picture." This concept was difficult for me to grasp because my world was the reserve and its boundaries. I had no working knowledge of what was happening on a broader scale. Many issues had no relevance because they did not affect me. I didn't understand the economics of everyday life and wasn't familiar with provincial or federal social policies. At that time, I cared only about aboriginal issues and fighting for the aboriginal cause. My vision was narrow and limited, and I struggled to broaden it.

I completed the YTC/GMCC Social Work program with a perfect grade point average. However, I was concerned about the equivalency between the YTC program and the on-campus program. I wondered if the content was the same and if I would have received the same marks if I had attended on-campus. I was assured many times that it was. Given these positive academic experiences, I decided to pursue a social work degree at University. One very special Grant MacEwan instructor helped me to expand my thinking and knowledge base. From day one, John Hutton challenged me to see things on a larger scale. He motivated me to think and to look at issues from a different perspective. He brought me out of the isolated world that was my frame of reference and encouraged me to pursue my future education. He tutored me through the tough courses and provided motivation, encouragement, and support during difficult times.

Soon after I started the B.S.W. program, I discovered that the university was very different from the nurturing, safe environment I had experienced at GMCC. The classes were considerably larger, and I felt out of place. At that time, only four aboriginal students were registered in the B.S.W. program: me, two students who were in their last year, and another student who was just starting. The course content was presented in a way that I was unaccustomed to, and the atmosphere was so strange and different. Many times during the first year I felt that I did not belong there, that I was not smart enough and I would never be able to pass these courses. I longed for what I had at YTC and it was a day-to-day struggle not to quit. My faith in my academic abilities was crushed when I went from straight A's to C's. I was devastated when I had to repeat two first-year courses. In spite of all my doubts, I persevered, and in my last year, I regained my self-esteem and was anxious to participate in the field practicum. Because of the GMCC program I knew my strengths were in this area. I had the "hands on" experience and could apply the social work methods and practices to my practicum.

Reflecting back, I do not regret the experiences I had. I believe that all of my doubts and insecurities helped to heighten my sense of accomplishment when I finally received my Bachelor of Social Work Degree. I know how hard I had to work and the many sacrifices I had to make in order to achieve this goal. Without these sacrifices, I believe the degree would not have meant as much, nor would I feel as strongly as I do today about social work and being a professional social worker. I have made a personal commitment to abide by the *Social Work Code of Ethics* in both my professional and my personal life. I have to practice what I preach. I live my life in a goldfish bowl! I have to be successful. Native people look to me to be a leader, whether I want to be or not.

The YTC/GMCC Social Work program for aboriginal students is much more than just a two-year academic diploma program. It provides mature Native students with the tools they need to begin to heal themselves first so that they can then help others. This program helps them to balance their personal growth and development with their learning so that they can graduate as highly skilled social work practitioners.

I commend Grant MacEwan Community College for its initiative in bringing such a curriculum to aboriginal communities. The Outreach program is innovative and provides a good foundation for those who want to pursue careers in social work. Everyone involved in the program worked hard to make it a success. It was the starting point for many of us to continue on with our learning.

Throughout our studies, the need for trained aboriginal social workers became evident. Many private troubles and public issues face aboriginal people today. Aboriginal children still comprise more than half of all the children in the Child Welfare system. Social issues such as alcoholism, sexual abuse, family violence, and suicide have not decreased. Aboriginal people are still struggling to survive assimilation and discrimination. At the present time, many changes are happening for aboriginal people at the national level. Politically, there is a more concerted movement toward self-government and self-determination. If Native people are going to take charge of their future, they will need many more trained aboriginals to work in all areas of the social work profession.

A New Vision

by Barbara Beaulieu

Since I was 16 years old I wanted to be a social worker. Part of my dream came true when I worked as a Band social worker for the Dene Tha Band. The only problem was I didn't have a diploma.

When Grant MacEwan Community College's Social Work Outreach Program came to High Level (about 738 km north of Edmonton), I applied and was accepted. I thought I would simply go to the classes, get my diploma, and go back to work for the Band. Little did I realize that that experience would change my life.

A part of me knew that my people were suffering. However, I did not realize the extent of these problems or how they were all connected. The unemployment, the alcoholism, the family violence, the sexual and physical abuse were all there, right in front of me, but I could not see them. This program opened my eyes, my heart, and my mind.

One of the elements in the program was the morning circle and prayer. It became a vital part of the students' academic life. It gave us a chance to consider our problems for the day and to concentrate on our school work. We prayed for guidance and support from our fellow classmates as well as from the Great Spirit. The circle also gave us a safe place to release our anger and pain when we were dealing with difficult subjects such as sexual abuse and the colonization of Native people. The smudging and prayers gave us back our faith and renewed our hope for ourselves and others. They helped heal the hurt and anger we felt when we dealt with the effects of the assimilation and integration of Natives into the mainstream society.

The personal development sessions were another important component of the program. We learned that the best thing we can do to help others is to deal with our own personal issues first. I believe that without those sessions we could not have become truly aware of ourselves or who we were. I found this part of the program the most difficult because it made me look at painful incidents and re-live them again. However, in the end, I felt better. I found I didn't have to waste my energy trying to keep these memories suppressed. They don't look so big and scary to me any more.

One of the best memories I have of our class is how we all pulled together and helped each other through rough spots. We dealt with deaths, suicides, and illnesses; we would stop for a day or two, then get back to work. We also experienced happy events—two marriages and seven births.

We were also fortunate to have instructors who really shared their work and lives with us. Dr. Apela Colorado, Vi Cerezke-Schooler, Kim Zapf, and Greg Poelzer worked hard to make this program successful. They shared with us their passion for social work and for helping others.

One of the hardest courses was the one that dealt with child sexual abuse. It always left us emotionally drained at the end of the day. Often, we would joke and laugh just to break the tension in the room. Vi's understanding helped us deal with our feelings.

The most interesting course was Political Science. Greg's way of presenting this material also allowed us to explore our feelings about certain issues—our anger, our frustration, and our hope for the Native peoples of Canada. One class was held at the Dene Tha reserve where we talked to the Band leaders and had a tea dance at the end of the day. We did a survey about Native politics, and the class all worked together to get it done.

There was only one man in our class and I'm sure he found it difficult at times, but there was also fun and laughter. Once, when Kim Zapf asked, "When does engagement start?" our lone male student replied, "When you give her a ring."

I found this learning experience to be very rewarding. It is one I will never forget.

In Retrospect

by Priscilla Lalonde

"Of all the teachings we receive
This one is most important,
Nothing belongs to you
Of what there is,
Of what you take
You must share."

Chief Dan George

I am honored to be asked to share with you my learning experiences from college and university. In order to do so, I must first describe my personal experiences, and tell how these experiences have intertwined with who I am and how they influenced the way I handled college and university.

I grew up in a small northern community comprised primarily of Native people. As a young Native person, I had very little experience or understanding of anything beyond the community in which I lived. Day-to-day living was very much a part of my culture.

My family moved to a larger town when I was seventeen. It was there that I learned about racism and discrimination. Because of who I was, there were many situations where I was treated as less than a person. Such social attitudes can certainly cause a person to question his or her self-identity. Fortunately, I had a family who supported their children and encouraged us to be proud of who we were.

I was working as an addictions counsellor trainee when I first heard about the Grant MacEwan Community College (GMCC) Social Work Outreach Program. From 1981 to 1982, I attended the first-year of the program at the Alberta Vocational Centre (AVC) Grouard. The College offered courses one week a month so that students could work and continue with their education.

The program provided me with many opportunities. It allowed me to see beyond a day-to-day existence and experience a broader world view. I learned that I could make choices. The group members taught me to trust and to support others, and most importantly, the Social Work Program gave me the opportunity to explore who I was as a person and what I needed to learn in order to work effectively with people.

The first year of this program was a time of major personal growth, and I enjoyed learning from both the instructors and the other students. As a group, we learned to build a trusting and open environment in which we could share our personal concerns. This ability to share strengthened us as individuals. The strength and courage I received then allowed me to continue with my education.

I completed the first year of the program in 1982 and decided to attend the second year in Edmonton. It was the first time that I had ever left my family and community for any great length of time. Although I experienced "culture shock," I was able to adjust fairly quickly because the College was small and I could travel home. One of my greatest supports came from another Native student who was in the same program. During the course of that second year, I was able to confirm, within myself, that social work was my chosen career. I was able to retain and appreciate the philosophical base that came from my culture as well as learn and integrate new concepts.

When I received my Social Services Worker Diploma in 1983, I felt I had achieved a major accomplishment. At the time, very few Native students chose to complete their education and return to their communities. If the GMCC Outreach Program had not been available, I believe I may not have completed my education either. Many Native students chose not to leave their rural communities, and the Outreach program allowed them to stay with their families and attend classes. Families are extremely important to Natives, and to leave one's family is to leave behind a part of yourself. When I left home to attend the program in Edmonton, I felt a strong sense of isolation and fear, but because of what I learned in the first year of the program, I found I had the strength to continue.

I continued working in the social work field until 1988. At that time, I decided to continue my formal education and was subsequently accepted into the Bachelor of Social Work Program at the University of Calgary. When I started classes,

I discovered that I was only one of two Native students who had been accepted into the third year of the program. University was a particularly challenging experience for me. In the first semester I considered quitting many times. I received subtle messages from some professors that caused me to question my abilities. For example, I heard that, as a Native student, I would probably have a difficult time at University because I was at an "academic disadvantage." Also, students who had a community college background would not do as well as students who came from another university program. I felt very isolated and incapable of completing the course work required. The atmosphere of the university was totally different from my college experience. However, during one class I heard a quote by Nietzsche that stayed with me and summarized my university experience: "What will not destroy me, will make me stronger." I repeated these words to myself many times. When I finally graduated in 1990, I indeed felt stronger for having successfully met the challenge and keeping my beliefs and values intact.

The experience of attending college and university was enlightening in many ways. In college, I learned about myself and how I fit into the field of social work. In university, I learned to "play the game" in order to succeed. The two experiences did not quite connect with each other. The college program could have prepared me better for the requirements of a university B.S.W. program. I discovered I was missing critical preparatory courses such as statistics and research methodology, which would have helped enormously.

In university, many courses emphasized professional development, but they gave no consideration to personal development. I met students who had completed their B.S.W. degree and then found themselves trying to deal with personal issues that had not been addressed once over the course of four years. The university program had not provided them with the tools they needed to deal with their personal problems. After working in the social work field, I know that who I am relates directly to the manner in which I work with my clients.

In retrospect, I would not have forgone either experience. Both left me with new skills and an opportunity to meet many wonderful people. I thank the Creator for giving me these experiences, and I hope that others will also have the chance to continue with their education. I would like other Native students to know that with strength and determination, they too could complete either program, and then offer their new skills to the people in their communities.

O Great Spirit

Whose voice I hear in the winds
And whose breath gives life to all the world.

Hear me! I am small and weak
I need your strength and wisdom.

Let me walk in beauty and make my eyes
Ever behold the red and purple sunset.

Make my hands respect the things you
Have made and my ears sharp to hear your voice.

Make me wise so that I may understand
The things you have taught my people

Let me learn the lessons you have hidden in every
leaf and rock.

I seek strength, not to be greater than my brother
but to fight my greatest enemy – myself.

Make me always ready to come to you with
Clean hands and straight eyes.

So that when life fades as the fading sunset
My spirit may come to you
Without shame.

Author Unknown

A Chronology of GMCC's Social Work Outreach Programs

Name & Dates of Program	Courses Offered	Sponsoring Group
Hobbema		
Jan./78 – Spring/80	1st year	Dept. of Indian Affairs & Northern Development
Ft. McLeod		
Group A Mar./77 – Dec./79	1st year	Department of Indian Affairs & Northern Development
Group B Apr./77 – Dec./79		
Nechi		
1978 – 1980	Individual courses only	Nechi Institute
Northlands		
1979 – 1985	1st year courses. (mostly delivered summers)	Northlands School Division
1981 – 1982	1st year	
Fort Smith		
1979 – 1981	1st year	Arctic College
Yukon		
Fall/78 – Mar./80	1st year	Dept. of Indian & Inuit Affairs, C.E.I.C., Yukon Territory Gov't.

Appendix 1

Name & Dates of Program	Courses Offered	Sponsoring Group
Slave Lake		
Sept./83 – June/84	1st year	Lesser Slave Lake Regional Council
Blue Quills		
Group 1 Jan./84 – Dec./85	1st & 2nd year	Blue Quills First Nations College
Group 2 Sept./85 – June/87		
Group 3 Sept./87 – June/89		
Group 4 Sept./89 – June 91		
Grouard		
Group 1 Sept./86 – June/88	1st & 2nd year	A.V.C. Grouard
Group 2 Sept./88 – June/90		
Group 3 Sept./90 – June/92	1st & 2nd year	A.V.C. Lesser Slave Lake
Group 4 Sept./92 – on		
Slave Lake		
Group 1 Sept./92 – on	2nd year	A.V.C. Lesser Lake Lake
Yellowhead Tribal Council		
Group 1 Nov./86 – Dec./88	1st & 2nd year	Yellowhead Tribal Council, C.E.I.C., Indian & Northern Affairs
Group 2 Jan./89 – Sept./90		
Group 3 Sept./92 – on		
High Level		
Aug./90 – Dec./90	Foundation program	C.E.I.C.
Jan./91 – Dec./92	1st & 2nd year	High Level Tribal Council, C.E.I.C.

A Chronology of GMCC's Social Work Outreach Programs

Name & Dates of Program	Courses Offered	Sponsoring Group
Onion Lake Aug./91 – Dec./91	Four courses	Lakeland College

In addition three other outreach programs were delivered which did not focus on aboriginal people, although the first two did include a few aboriginal students. All programs reflected the same philosophic thrust.

Name & Dates of Program	Courses Offered	Sponsoring Group
Yellowhead Regional Consortium		
Group 1 Sept./87 – June/89	1st & 2nd Year	Yellowhead Consortium
Group 2 Sept./91 – on		
Pembina Consortium		
Jan./92 – on	1st & 2nd year	Pembina Consortium
Mennonite Centre Project		
Jan./90 – Dec./90	1st & $1/2$ of 2nd year, completed 2nd year 1991 as part of regular on-campus program	Canada Manpower & Immigration, Mennonite Centre for Newcomers

The Social Work Program has offered an on-campus 2nd year program since 1967. The Program began at the Northern Alberta Institute of Technology and in 1972 moved to the newly built Millwoods Campus of Grant MacEwan Community College. Since 1980 an evening program focusing on students already working in the field, has also been available. Mostly 1st year classes have been offered and students have to transfer to the regular on-campus program to complete their courses. The Social Work Program is now located at GMCC's new City Centre Campus in Edmonton.

Outreach Program Locations

High Level

Grouard

Slave Lake

St. Paul

Onion Lake

Edson

Spruce Grove • Edmonton

Hinton

Drayton Valley

Hobbema

Since 1978 Grant MacEwan Community College has offered social work outreach programs at these sites in Alberta. Programs have also been offered at sites in the Yukon and North West Territories.

Fort McLeod

Author's Biographies

Barbara Beaulieu

Barbara Beaulieu graduated from the Grant MacEwan Community College (GMCC) Social Work Program at High Level, Alberta in January 1993. While in the program, Barbara, who is a member of the Dene Tha Band, was class President and was also awarded the John Hutton Scholarship for Social Policy and Social Action.

Before entering the program, Barbara was a Band social worker. Since graduating Barbara has returned to her former position where she feels the skills she has developed have greatly enhanced her practice.

Barbara Beaulieu has four children, two boys and two girls.

Pam Colorado

Pam has been an assistant professor at the University of Calgary, Faculty of Social Work for several years. She obtained a Bachelor of Science in 1971 and a Master of Science degree in 1975 from the University of Wisconsin. She has undertaken Special Studies at Harvard University, and in 1984, received a PhD in Social Welfare from Brandeis University, Boston. She was also a Ford Foundation Fellow from 1975 to 1978. Universities at which she has lectured include McMaster, Lethbridge, Alaska, and Wisconsin.

Pam, who is an aboriginal person, has been a popular workshop presenter internationally, and has researched and written extensively about Native issues. Pam is currently the coordinator of the Worldwide Indigenous Science Network. She has two children.

Kay Feehan

Kay Feehan received her Bachelor of Arts from the University of Saskatchewan, a Bachelor of Social Work from the University of Manitoba, and a Master of Social Work from the University of Calgary. In 1989, she was awarded an honorary doctorate degree from St. Stephen's Theological College, Edmonton. She is a Registered Social Worker in Alberta and has held several social work positions in Saskatoon, Prince Albert, and Edmonton. Kay has worked in hospital settings and in the child welfare area. Kay joined Grant MacEwan Community College in 1974 and has been Chair of the College's Social Work Program for more than 17 years. She has also been active on several community and hospital boards; co-founded the Terra School for Unmarried Mothers, and Acadia House for Emotionally Disturbed Youth. She was also instrumental in the development of the Social Work Outreach programs at Grant MacEwan Community College. Kay's husband Bernard is a justice on the Court of Queen's Bench of Alberta. They have seven children and 13 grandchildren.

Sophie Freud

Sophie Freud is a Professor Emerita of Simmons College School of Social Work. She received a French Baccalaureate in Casablanca, AB cum laude at Radcliffe College, a Master of Social Work from Simmons College, and a doctoral degree from Brandeis University. Many of her published articles, books, and book reviews have dealt with the psychology of women, psychotherapy, passion, psychological theories, and the education of mental health professionals. Dr. Freud has practiced psychiatric social work, worked as a consultant, presented at scholarly gatherings, and taught for many years. She feels, however, that her teaching experience in northern Canada was one of the highlights of her extensive career. Sophie is the granddaughter of Sigmund Freud and the mother of three children.

David Hannis

David Hannis has a background in community organization, social planning, social policy analysis, clinical social work, and adult education. Since 1984, he has taught in the Social Work Program at Grant MacEwan Community College.

David Hannis was trained in England at the universities of Exeter, York, and Leeds and received a Canadian Master of Social Work equivalency in 1974. He has worked and travelled extensively, and since moving to Canada in 1975, has held several positions with municipal and provincial government social service departments. He is also a Registered Social Worker in Alberta. David has a graduate Diploma in Education from the University of Alberta with emphasis on Intercultural Education, and is currently continuing studies in the area of adult learning and community development at that same university.

David has benefitted from the wisdom of many good teachers in his life, but has learned the most from his two daughters, Katherine and Kristina. He is married to a social worker, Carol Cass.

Priscilla Lalonde

Priscilla Lalonde graduated from the Grant MacEwan Community College Social Work Program in 1983, and in 1990, she received her Bachelor of Social Work degree from the University of Calgary. A Treaty Indian from the Driftpile Reserve in Alberta, Priscilla Lalonde has had extensive experience as an addictions counsellor, a child welfare worker, and a child welfare casework supervisor. She is currently the Director of the Sucker Creek Women's Emergency Shelter.

Priscilla has two children, Marisa and Skyler, who give her much joy and inspiration.

Carolyn Peacock

Carolyn Peacock is an aboriginal social worker with a background in early childhood development and social work. For ten years, she worked as the Director of a daycare center on the Enoch Reserve in Alberta. She was also a Band child welfare worker and Band child welfare manager before she entered the Grant MacEwan Community College/Yellowhead Tribal Council Social Work Program in 1986. She graduated from that program with a Diploma in Social Work in 1988 and obtained her Bachelor of Social Work from the University of Calgary in 1991. She is a Registered Social Worker in Alberta. Carolyn is currently employed as the program supervisor, Yellowhead Tribal Services Agency, and works primarily in the area of child welfare.

She is married and has four children, Shane, Jason, Jessi, and Kimberly.

William Pelech

William was the Coordinator of the Grant MacEwan Community College Social Work Program in High Level, Alberta from July 1990 to January 1993. He has a Bachelor of Social Work (1st class) from the University of Victoria and two years Arts training at the Vancouver Community College. William has extensive experience working with aboriginal people. For five years he was the Coordinator of the Dene Tha Social Development Program, and before that he worked as a consultant to the Little Red River Band. He has also worked with the Department of Indian Affairs in St. Paul, Alberta, and as a Parent Counsellor in British Columbia. William has two children.

Gino Restivo

Gino Restivo has a Bachelor of Arts from McMaster University and a Master of Social Work from Waterloo Lutheran (now Wilfrid Laurier) University. He is a Registered Social Worker in Alberta, with extensive practical experience. In the almost twenty years since completing his Master's degree, Gino has worked at a Detention Centre Clinic; at the Oxford Mental Health Centre in Woodstock, Ontario; at Newham Social Services in London, England; at the Hamilton Children's Aid Society in Rankin Inlet in the North West Territories; for Alberta Family and Community Services; and for the Edmonton Public School Board as a social work consultant.

For the past six years, Gino Restivo has been employed at the Yellowhead Tribal Council (YTC) as the Coordinator of the Grant MacEwan Community College Social Work Program, and as the YTC Coordinator of the Bachelor of Social Work program delivered by the University of Calgary.

Gino Restivo is married to a social worker, Alice Buie. They have three children, Brent, Lee, and Vanessa, who provide Gino with his 'raison d'être' and act as a check on his reality.

Doug Smith

Doug Smith was the Coordinator of the Grant MacEwan Community College Social Work Program at Blue Quills First Nation's College in St. Paul, Alberta from 1983 to 1990. He has a Bachelor of Arts in English and History from the University of Alberta, Edmonton as well as a Master of Arts in History from the same university. He also has a Master of Arts in Social Welfare Policy from McMaster University in Hamilton, and from 1973 to 1975, was a doctoral candidate at Queens University, Kingston. He is a Registered Social Worker in Alberta.

Doug has extensive experience as a social worker and has been employed by the governments of Ontario and Alberta in the areas of rehabilitation, child welfare, and income security. Doug lives in Edmonton and has one son, Mark.

Marianne Wright

Marianne is a social worker in private practice in Edmonton and an instructor at Grant MacEwan Community College. She began her career over 25 years ago and has held social work positions in the United States, eastern Canada, and Edmonton. She has worked in the areas of income security, child welfare, hospital social work and non-medical psychotherapy. She received her Bachelor of Arts from the University of Oregon and a Bachelor of Social Work and a Master of Arts in Social Work from the University of Calgary. She began her private practice in 1978 and her teaching career at Grant MacEwan Community College in 1979.

Marianne has been active on several community boards and has co-edited a social work textbook. Marianne's husband Jim is an economist, they have two children.

Michael Kim Zapf

Kim Zapf has a Bachelor of Arts from the University of Waterloo, a Master of Social Work from the University of British Columbia, and a PhD in Social Work from the University of Toronto. Dr. Zapf has published numerous articles on rural and northern social work practice issues and has contributed to several social work texts. He has also presented at conferences in Canada, the U.S.A., Sweden, and Finland.

Kim is currently an Associate Professor with the Faculty of Social Work at the University of Calgary. From 1976 to 1982, he worked in the Yukon Territory as a Probation Officer, a Senior Probation Officer, and Director of Community Corrections. He has also taught and learned from Native students in both the Grant MacEwan Community College Social Work Outreach Program in High Level, Alberta, and the University of Calgary Aboriginal Bachelor of Social Work Program with the Yellowhead Tribal Council, Spruce Grove, Alberta.

In addition to his academic role, Kim also performs in an amateur magic show as 'The Great Takhini' and often incorporates magic into his cross-cultural teaching.

Kim is married to Dr. Penny Ford and lives in Calgary.